Graceful Living

Experience a life of freedom and joy!

Discover who Christ is, what he has done for us on the cross, and your new identity and way of living in Him—a life of freedom and joy!

MELANIE NEWTON

JOYFUL
WALK
BIBLE
STUDIES

We extend our heartfelt thanks to Tim Stevenson who created the original T.E.A.M. Training course upon which the core of this study is based. We also appreciate the many women who served as editors for the original version of this study guide—Brenda Sharp, Dawn Paradise, Rita Geismar, Samantha Smith, Lana Schara, Michelle Burns, Hannah Ware, Pat Archer, and Joye Messerli. Without your help, we would never have accomplished this monumental task in a timely manner.

Graceful Living: Experience a life of freedom and joy

© 2025 by Melanie Newton. All rights reserved.

Published by Joyful Walk Press. Flower Mound, TX.

ISBN: 979-8-9925303-9-1

For questions about the use of this study guide or for bulk orders, please email us at melanienewton.com/contact.

Cover graphic is a public domain image accessed at pixabay.com/photos/landscape-sunrise-swans-sun-2025238. Swans are a natural illustration of graceful living. They are graceful creatures, live faithfully in community with other swans, and become new creations as they are transformed from awkward "ugly ducklings" to beautiful mature birds.

Melanie Newton is the author of "Graceful Beginnings" books for anyone new to the Bible and "Joyful Walk Bible Studies" for established Christians. Her mission is to help women learn to study the Bible for themselves and to grow their Bible-teaching skills to lead others.

Joyful Walk Bible Studies are grace-based studies for women of all ages. Each study guide follows the inductive method of Bible study (observation, interpretation, application) in a warm and inviting format.

We pray that you and your group will find *Graceful Living* a resource that God will use to strengthen you in your faith walk with God.

Christ-Focused • Grace-Based • Bible-Rich

JOYFUL WALK PRESS
Flower Mound, TX

MELANIE NEWTON

Melanie Newton is a Louisiana girl who made the choice to follow Jesus while attending LSU. She and her husband Ron married and moved to Texas for him to attend Dallas Theological Seminary. They stayed in Texas where Ron led a wilderness camping ministry for troubled youth for many years. Ron now helps corporations with their challenging employees and is the author of the top-rated business book, *No Jerks on the Job*.

Melanie jumped into raising three Texas-born children and serving in ministry to women at her church. Through the years, the Lord has given her opportunity to do Bible teaching and to write grace-based Bible studies for women that are now available from her website (melanienewton.com) and on Bible.org. *Graceful Beginnings* books are for anyone new to the Bible. *Joyful Walk Bible Studies* are for maturing Christians.

Melanie is a speaker, author, and trainer with Joyful Walk Ministries. Her mission is to help women learn to study the Bible for themselves and to grow their Bible-teaching skills to lead others. Her heart's desire is to encourage you to have a joyful relationship with Jesus Christ so you are willing to share that experience with others around you.

"Jesus took hold of me in 1972, and I've been on this great adventure ever since. My life is a gift of God, full of blessings in the midst of difficult challenges. The more I have learned and experienced God's absolutely amazing grace, the more I have discovered my faith walk to be a joyful one. I'm still seeking that joyful walk every day..."

Melanie

OTHER BIBLE STUDIES BY MELANIE NEWTON

Graceful Beginnings books for anyone new to the Bible:

A Fresh Start (basics for new Christians)
Painting the Portrait of Jesus (the Gospel of John)
The God You Can Know (the character of God)
Grace Overflowing (an overview of Paul's 13 letters)
The Walk from Fear to Faith (Old Testament women)
Satisfied by His Love (women who knew Jesus)
Seek the Treasure (study of Ephesians)
Pathways to a Joyful Walk (6 pathways to a joy-filled life)

Joyful Walk Bible Studies for growing Christians:

Adorn Yourself with Godliness (1 Timothy and Titus, also in Spanish)
Everyday Women, Ever Faithful God (Old Testament women, also in Spanish)
Connecting Faith to Life on Planet Earth (Genesis 1-11; Revelation)
Graceful Living (the essentials for a grace-based Christian life)
Graceful Living Today (a devotional journal for a joyful life)
Healthy Living (Colossians and Philemon)
Heartbreak to Hope (the Gospel of Mark)
Identity: Sticking to Your Faith in a Pull-Apart World (Ezra thru Malachi)
Knowing Jesus, Knowing Joy (Philippians, also in Spanish)
Live Out His Love (New Testament women)
Perspective (1 and 2 Thessalonians)
Profiles of Perseverance (Old Testament men, also in Spanish)
Radical Acts (Acts)
Reboot, Renew, Rejoice (1 and 2 Chronicles)
The God-Dependent Woman (2 Corinthians)
To Be Found Faithful (2 Timothy)

Resources for Leading Others

Be a Christ-Focused Small Group Leader
Leap into Lifestyle Disciplemaking
Bible Study Leadership Made Easy (online video course)
Painting the Picture of Jesus (the "I Am's" of Jesus lessons for children)
Teaching Children the God They Can Know (the character of God for children)

Download our catalogue and get resources for your spiritual growth at melanienewton.com.

Contents

Using This Study Guide

This study guide consists of 11 lessons covering foundational principles of Christianity — who Christ is, what he accomplished on the cross for us, what his resurrection means for us, and our identity in him.

As a topical study, the lessons cover a lot of different scripture passages. Because of the importance of clearly communicating the truth of our faith in Christ, each lesson contains several paragraphs of teaching interspersed between the questions.

The lessons are divided into 5 sections (about 25 minutes in length). The first 4 sections contain a detail study of the passages. The last section is a podcast that provides additional insight to the lesson.

If you cannot do the entire lesson one week, please read through the "Day One Study" of the lesson and listen to the podcast.

THE BASIC STUDY

This study is a topical study rather than covering one section of the Bible. That means you will be looking at multiple passages of Scripture in each lesson.

Yet, the lessons include core questions that will take you through the process of inductive Bible study—observation, interpretation, and application. The process is more easily understood in the context of answering these questions:

- What does the passage say? (Observation: what is actually there)

- What does it mean? (Interpretation: the author's intended meaning)

- How does this apply to me today? (Application: making it personal) *Graceful Living* questions are the application questions in this study. These questions lead you to introspection and application of specific truths to your life.

STUDY ENHANCEMENTS

Deeper Discoveries (optional): Embedded within the sections are *optional* questions for research of subjects we don't have time to cover adequately in the lessons or contain information that significantly enhance the basic study. If you are meeting with a small group, your leader may give you the opportunity to share your "discoveries."

Study Aids: To aid in proper interpretation and application of the study, five additional study aids are located where appropriate in the lesson:

- Historical Insight

- Scriptural Insight

- From the Greek/Hebrew (definitions of Greek or Hebrew words)

- Focus on the Meaning

- Think About It (thoughtful reflection)

- Dependent Living (illustrating what it means to live dependently on God)

Other useful study tools: Use online tools or apps (blueletterbible.org or "Blue Letter Bible app" is especially helpful) to find *cross references* (verses with similar content to what you are studying) and meanings of the *original Greek words or phrases* used (usually called "interlinear"). You can also look at any verse in *various Bible translations* to help with understanding what it is saying. Feel free to add your own study at the end of each lesson.

PODCASTS

Find podcasts coordinating with these lessons at melanienewton.com/podcasts (choose "9: Graceful Living). Or you can read blogs similar to the podcasts at melanienewton.com/blog. Listen to the first podcast as an introduction to the study.

NEW TESTAMENT SUMMARY

The New Testament opens with the births of John and Jesus. About 30 years later, John challenged the Jews to indicate their repentance (turning from sin and toward God) by submitting to water baptism—a familiar Old Testament practice used for repentance as well as when a Gentile converted to Judaism (to be washed clean of idolatry).

Jesus, God's incarnate Son, publicly showed the world what God is like and taught his perfect ways for 3 – 3½ years. After preparing 12 disciples to continue Christ's earthly work, he died voluntarily on a cross for mankind's sin, rose from the dead, and returned to heaven. The account of his earthly life is recorded in 4 books known as the Gospels (the biblical books of Matthew, Mark, Luke and John named after the compiler of each account).

After Jesus' return to heaven, the followers of Christ were then empowered by the Holy Spirit and spread God's salvation message among the Jews, a number of whom believed in Christ. The apostle Paul and others carried the good news to the Gentiles during 3 missionary journeys (much of this recorded in the book of Acts). Paul wrote 13 New Testament letters to churches & individuals (Romans through Philemon). The section in our Bible from Hebrews to Jude contains 8 additional letters penned by five men, including two apostles (Peter and John) and two of Jesus' half-brothers (James and Jude). The author of Hebrews is unknown. The apostle John also recorded Revelation, which summarizes God's final program for the world. The Bible ends as it began—with a new, sinless creation.

GRACEFUL LIVING

When it comes to knowing who I am and where I stand with God, the best course I have ever taken was TEAM Training, created by Tim Stevenson as he pastored a church in the DFW area. I found that this course effectively covered the foundational principles of Christianity—who Christ is, what he accomplished on the cross for us, what the resurrection means for us, and our identity in him. It communicated clearly and succinctly to me what I needed to know to live dependently on Christ and rest in my assurance of life in him and through him. Through this course, I learned more about the purpose for the cross and the resurrection than I had ever heard before. I learned how to recognize the poison of legalism in a Christian's life. I also became aware that my flesh is not getting better the longer I know Christ. I need to depend 100% on him now as I ever did as a young believer in the 70s. Hundreds of others also found their lives transformed as they understood God's grace toward them and active in their lives. They, too, experienced a life of freedom and joy!

Times change; people change; circumstances change. That course is no longer being taught. Yet, these truths are essential for every believer to enjoy the life God has planned for her. So I have adapted the course (given as a series of lectures) to a women's Bible study. The outline of the study is based on what was taught in the original course. I have revised a lot of the wording to make it more relatable and added information where needed to make the studies flow better.

The heart of the course has remained the same—the message of God's love and grace in Jesus Christ and the reality of "Christ alive and living in me." Understanding God's grace given to you is essential to enjoying the life that God has planned for you.

May our "Grace-giving" God completely fill your heart with his grace so that you become a "Grace-giver" in your life. "Graceful living" is a life overflowing with his grace—**a life of freedom and joy!**

Note: If you look at the cover image of this study, you will see a group of swans. Swans are a natural illustration of graceful living. They are graceful creatures, live faithfully in community with other swans, and become "new creations" as they are transformed from awkward "ugly ducklings" to beautiful mature birds.

DISCUSSION GROUP GUIDELINES

Anyone can do this study alone. If you are doing this as part of a group, we suggest you use the following guidelines to maintain a safe environment for your group members to learn together.

1. **Attend consistently** whether your lesson is done or not. You will learn from the other women, and they want to get to know you.

2. **Set aside time** to work through the study questions. The goal of Bible study is to get to know Jesus. He will change your life.

3. **Share your insights** from your personal study time. As you spend time in the Bible, Jesus will teach you truth through his Spirit inside you.

4. **Respect each other's insights**. Listen thoughtfully. Encourage each other as you interact. Refrain from dominating the discussion if you have a tendency to be talkative. ☺

5. **Celebrate our unity** in Christ. Avoid bringing up controversial subjects such as politics, divisive issues, and denominational differences.

6. **Maintain confidentiality.** Remember that anything shared during the group time is not to leave the **group** (unless permission is granted by the one sharing).

7. **Pray for one another** as sisters in Christ.

8. **Get to know the women** in your group. Please do not use your small group members for solicitation purposes for home businesses, though.

There is a small group discussion guide available at the end of this study. Anyone can use the guide to lead a group through a discussion of the questions in this study. This is especially useful for groups that have less than two hours to meet together.

Enjoy your Joyful Walk Bible Study!

Recommended: Listen to the podcast "The Promise of Graceful Living" before doing the first lesson as an introduction to the whole study.

The Promise of Graceful Living

WHAT IS GRACE?

- Biblical grace is God giving favor to someone, not because they are good enough to deserve it but because His love chooses to do so. God's grace springs from God's love.

- The Bible says that God's grace is so abundant it is like a cup overflowing. *1 Timothy 1:13-14*

- God's invitation to you and your acceptance of it is wrapped up in one phrase—by grace you are saved through faith.

BY GRACE YOU ARE SAVED THROUGH FAITH

"For it is by grace you have been saved, through faith—and this not from yourselves, it is the gift of God—not by works, so that no one can boast." (Ephesians 2:8-9)

By grace you are saved through faith. Three important words in that phrase explain the basis of your salvation and why you can be confident in it—grace, saved, and faith.

God gives His GRACE.

- Biblical grace is God giving favor to someone, not because they are good enough to deserve it but because His love chooses to do so. Grace is a free gift from God that you accepted when you received Christ through faith. *Ephesians 2:4-5*

- Our faith begins with receiving the love of God and understanding it in the Gospel. We start with how much God loves us. Then, we see His love in His grace to us. *1 John 4:19*

- God's grace is His undeserved favor abundantly poured out on those who desperately need Him and respond to Him by faith.

By God's grace, you are SAVED.

- To be saved means "to be rescued, spared from disaster." When you receive Christ, you are rescued from God's wrath against sin and eternal separation from God.

- You can know that you have a secure and personal relationship with God because you are saved through faith in Jesus Christ.

You are saved, through FAITH in Jesus Christ.

- Faith is placing your trust in God and His Word. It is a full commitment to Christ.

- It is by faith alone that you are saved. *Ephesians 2:9*

- If you were standing before God and He asked you, "Why should I let you into my heaven?" Now, you can say, "I know I am saved by your grace through my faith in your Son Jesus Christ." You are in!

When you trust in Christ for your salvation, God's grace is abundantly poured on you. And with that grace comes so many blessings and benefits.

THE PROMISE OF GRACEFUL LIVING

Graceful living is for everyone who has accepted God's gift of salvation through faith in Jesus Christ. Your salvation is an undeserved gift from God. You cannot earn it. You cannot win it. You only receive it by faith.

- "Graceful living" begins and continues through Jesus Christ. He gave His life for you by grace, so He could give His life to you by grace, so He could live His life through you by grace.

- "Graceful living" is life overflowing with His grace giving you rest from trying to earn God's favor. *Matthew 11:28-30*

- "Graceful living" is knowing Christ's love for you and letting that love motivate you to live for Him in obedience.

- "Graceful living" leads you to serve Christ through serving others. That is letting His life in you overflow to others around you, especially those who need to know Him.

- "Graceful living" is seeing your transformation from being a selfish, sinful being into having the likeness of Jesus Christ Himself. God's Holy Spirit does this to us from the inside out. We grow up into mature Christians who are beautiful in God's sight and bring His glory to everyone around us.

This *Graceful Living Bible Study* will help you build a foundation for successful, enjoyable Christian living based on God's **grace** to you and for you. Understanding God's grace given to you is essential to enjoying the life that God has planned for you. That is the promise of "Graceful Living."

Let Jesus satisfy your heart with His grace so that your life overflows with His grace every day. You will experience a life of freedom and joy!

1: Christ, the Grace-Gift

For from his fullness we have all received, grace upon grace. For the law was given through Moses; grace and truth came through Jesus Christ. (John 1:16-17)

Ask the Lord Jesus to speak to you through His Word each day. Tell Him you are listening.

DAY ONE STUDY

Jesus Christ presented himself as the answer to every need of the human heart. The New Testament writers unanimously taught the same. Multitudes of people throughout the centuries since have witnessed that he does indeed do what he promised for those who trust and follow him.

I have been a Jesus follower for more than 40 years now. Not once have I regretted that decision. I am a lifelong learner, a student of God's Word and my Lord's life. He teaches me in many ways.

Recently, someone asked me, "How has Jesus discipled you? What has made the most impact on your life?"

When it comes to knowing who I am and where I stand with God, the best teaching I have had was a course at my church that effectively covered the foundational principles of Christianity—who Christ is, what he accomplished on the cross for us, what the resurrection means for us, and our identity in him. It communicated clearly and succinctly to me what I needed to know to live dependently on Christ and rest in my assurance of life **in** him and **through** him. Then, I learned more about the purpose for the cross and the resurrection than I had ever known before. I learned how to recognize the poison of legalism in a Christian's life. It was through this teaching that I became aware that my flesh is not getting better the longer I know Christ. I need to depend 100% on him now as I ever did as a young believer. These timeless truths are essential for every believer to enjoy the life God has planned for them. So I have adapted the original teaching I received (given as a series of lectures) into this Bible study called *Graceful Living*.

The heart of *Graceful Living* is the message of God's love and grace in Jesus Christ and the reality of "Christ alive and living in me." This study will help you build a foundation for successful, enjoyable Christian living based on God's "**grace**" to you and for you. Understanding God's grace given to you is essential to enjoying the life that God has planned for you. As you apply these truths in your life, you will experience a life of freedom and joy.

God's invitation to a life of freedom and joy

1. Read John 10:10 and Matthew 11:28-30. What does Jesus promise to his followers?

> **Focus on the Meaning:** Full is not empty. Full means to have purpose and meaning. Full does not mean easy, though. Fullness means that even when we are weary and burdened (Matthew 28:28-30), we can go to him with open hands and receive the rest and guidance that he readily gives. Jesus' invitation says, "Come to me. Connect to me. Learn from me. Rest with me." That sounds pretty wonderful. Jesus Christ invites you to a life of fullness, freedom and joy. Are you interested?

2. Read John 8:31-32. What does Jesus promise to his followers?

Truth. It is critically important for anyone who knows Christ to have sound theology (rational, systematic understanding of God). Theology is inescapable. Any thoughts you have about God or information you receive about God is theology. You may not realize it, but you live according to your theology.

Anyone's theology can be based on truth or error. Truth and error lead to dramatically different results. If truth sets you free, then the opposite is also true. Error binds you. When you know the truth that is revealed to you in the Bible, you will experience freedom. With freedom comes a life of joy. Do you want a life of joy? Stand firmly on God's truth revealed to you in his Word, the Bible.

3. Read John 1:16-17. What do Jesus' followers receive?

What Jesus offers to you, as one of his followers, is a life **full of grace**. What is grace? In particular, what is God's grace?

> **Focus on the Meaning:** Grace is commonly defined as unmerited favor, an undeserved gift. It is God's gift to an undeserving humanity. God gives his grace because of his great love and mercy (Ephesians 2:4-7).

Would you like a life full of God's grace? You are in the right place!

Christianity is Christ

The New Testament opens with the births of John the Baptist and Jesus. About 30 years later, John challenged the Jews to indicate their repentance (turning from sin and toward God) by submitting to water baptism—a familiar Old Testament practice used for repentance. It was also used when a non-Jew (usually called Gentile) converted to Judaism (to be washed clean of idolatry).

Shortly after that, Jesus presented himself to the public. The account of his earthly life is recorded in 4 books known as the Gospels, the biblical books of Matthew, Mark, Luke and John named after the compiler of each account. Each Gospel presents Jesus as "the Christ."

> **From the Greek:** This title "the Christ" is from the Greek word *christos,* a translation of the Hebrew term "Messiah" meaning "anointed one." The Old Testament prophets promised that the Messiah, as the anointed one of God, would come and do many wonderful things for God's people, including restoring God's Kingdom on earth. Christians are followers of Jesus, who is the Christ.

If you have heard the good news of the gospel and believed that Jesus is the Christ, the Son of God who gave himself for your sins, you have eternal life just by believing in him as your Savior. But more than salvation, Jesus Christ calls you into a relationship with himself.

Christianity is Christ! It is not a lifestyle, rules of conduct, or a society whose members were initiated by the sprinkling or covering of water. Christ calls all humans into a close relationship with him as brothers, sisters, and friends.

Yet, he is also our Lord, the one who sits at the right hand of his Father God as head over everything else in heaven and on earth. As Lord, Jesus Christ is our *master*—the one to whom we should willingly give our obedience. He is our *model* of how to live as humans in a dependent relationship with God, and he is our *mentor* in walking with us in that dependent relationship.

Jesus' disciples 2000 years ago were no different than we are except they physically beheld the risen Christ. We must see him through eyes of faith and allow the Gospels to leap off the page revealing our Lord. This is so that we may know this God-man who changed our lives as we received the Good News. We need to frequently read the Gospels, watch movies based on them, and tell the stories about Jesus as often as needed to know his life well because Christianity is Christ!

Through this study, you will get to know this Christ who is the ultimate grace gift to us.

4. ***Graceful Living:*** What questions do you have about Jesus or Christianity? Feel free to be honest here. God is faithful and has revealed so much that you can know for sure. Trust him to show you.

Respond to God in prayer about what he has shown you today.

DAY TWO STUDY—WHO IS JESUS?

According to the Bible, God chose to reveal himself to the nation of Israel and through Israel, to the world. Many truths about God ("attributes") are taught in the Old Testament. Our God is self-existent, all-powerful, all-knowing, present everywhere, holy, just, good, loving, and merciful.

But there is one thing clearly and relentlessly asserted about God in the Old Testament.

> *"Hear, 0 Israel! The LORD our God, **the LORD is one!** Love the LORD your God with all your heart and with all your soul and with all your strength." (Deuteronomy 6:4-5)*

Then, God himself spoke these words through Isaiah:

> *"You are my witnesses," declares the LORD, "and my servant whom I have chosen, so that you may know and believe me and understand that I am he. Before me no god was formed, nor will there be one after me. I, even I, am the LORD, and apart from me there is no savior." (Isaiah 43:10-11)*

Jesus of Nazareth presented himself to the people living in a very religious culture who held strongly to the belief that there is only one God. When Jesus came on the scene, he called people to a spiritual relationship with himself as well as with God the Father. It is no wonder that many of the Jewish leaders were appalled at what Jesus said. But Jesus demonstrated that what he claimed was indeed the truth.

Of all the world's religions, Jesus is the only "founder" who claimed to be equal with God. For the next few days, we will see what the scripture says about who Jesus Christ is.

What does the Bible say that Jesus claimed about himself? (Observation)

Let's look at what the Bible text says. Read the following verses from John 5. Mark the specific things that Jesus declares about himself. Then answer the question that follows.

So because Jesus was doing these things on the Sabbath, the Jewish leaders began to persecute him. In his defense Jesus said to them, "My Father is always at his work to this very day, and I too am working." For this reason, they tried all the more to kill him; not only was he breaking the Sabbath, but he was even calling God his own Father, making himself equal with God. (John 5:16-18)

Jesus gave them this answer: "Very truly I tell you, the Son can do nothing by himself; he can do only what he sees his Father doing, because whatever the Father does the Son also does. For the Father loves the Son and shows him all he does. Yes, and he will show him even greater works than these, so that you will be amazed. For just as the Father raises the dead and gives them life, even so the Son gives life to whom he is pleased to give it. Moreover, the Father judges no one, but has entrusted all judgment to the Son, that all may honor the Son just as they honor the Father. Whoever does not honor the Son does not honor the Father, who sent him. (John 5:19-23)

"Very truly I tell you, whoever hears my word and believes him who sent me has eternal life and will not be judged but has crossed over from death to life. Very truly I tell you, a time is coming and has now come when the dead will hear the voice of the Son of God and those who hear will live. For as the Father has life in himself, so He has granted the Son also to have life in himself. And he has given him authority to judge because he is the Son of Man. (John 5:24-27)

"I have testimony weightier than that of John [the Baptist]. For the works that the Father has given me to finish—the very works that I am doing—testify that the Father has sent me. And the Father who sent me has himself testified concerning me. You have never heard his voice nor seen his form, nor does his word dwell in you, for you do not believe the one he sent. You study the Scriptures diligently because you think that in them you have eternal life. These are the very Scriptures that testify about me, yet you refuse to come to me to have life." (John 5:36-40)

"But do not think I will accuse you before the Father. Your accuser is Moses, on whom your hopes are set. If you believed Moses, you would believe me, for he wrote about me." (John 5:45-46)

5. What does Jesus claim about himself in each of the following sections of John 5:16-47?

- Vv. 16-18—

- Vv. 19-23—

- Vv. 24-27—

- Vv. 36-40—

- Vv. 45-46—

In this "sermon," Jesus appeals to the audience to view the work he is doing as evidence that he has been sent by the Father (God). The Scriptures testify about him, and Moses himself wrote about him. Pretty strong claims! Like a lawyer trying a case, Jesus presents undeniable evidence that he is the promised Messiah who is the Son of God. He claimed and demonstrated that he was God in human flesh.

6. Jesus made more claims to rights and authority that are only associated with God. What right or authority does Jesus claim in the following passages?

- Mark 2:1-12—

- Luke 8:26-33—

- Luke 17:11-19—

- John 14:12-14—

Did you catch all that Jesus claimed and did that only God could or would do? Jesus was not just a good teacher. He claimed and demonstrated that he was God in human flesh.

7. Read John 6:35-40. What claims did Jesus make about himself?

- V. 35—

- Vv. 37-38—

- Vv. 39-40—

Not only does Jesus promise to meet the spiritual hunger and thirst of everyone who comes to him, but he also claims to have come down from heaven and to have been sent by God the Father. This is a claim of pre-existence, that is, Jesus is claiming to have existed before his human birth.

Jesus goes on to say that he has been sent by his Father to do the Father's will on earth. That will is to draw people to God and have authority over their eternal destiny. Only God has authority over eternal destiny. Jesus Christ claimed and demonstrated that he was God in human flesh.

8. *Graceful Living:* What did you learn about Jesus in the lesson today that you had not known before this study?

Respond to God in prayer about what he has shown you today.

DAY THREE STUDY

What does the Bible say that Jesus claimed about himself?

Let's look again at what the Bible text says. Read the following verses from John 8. Mark the specific things that Jesus declared about himself. Then answer the question that follows.

> *So Jesus said, "When you have lifted up the Son of Man, then you will know that I am he and that I do nothing on my own but speak just what the Father has taught me. The one who sent me is with me; he has not left me alone, for I always do what pleases him." (John 8:28-29)*

> *Jesus said to them, "If God were your Father, you would love me, for I have come here from God. I have not come on my own; God sent me. (John 8:42)*

> *Why is my language not clear to you? Because you are unable to hear what I say. You belong to your father, the devil, and you want to carry out your father's desires. He was a murderer from the beginning, not holding to the truth, for there is no truth in him. When he lies, he speaks his native language, for he is a liar and the father of lies. Yet because I tell the truth, you do not believe me! Can any of you prove me guilty of sin? If I am telling the truth, why don't you believe me? Whoever belongs to God hears what God says. The reason you do not hear is that you do not belong to God." (John 8:43-47)*

> *Jesus replied, "If I glorify myself, my glory means nothing. My Father, whom you claim as your God, is the one who glorifies me. Though you do not know him, I know him. If I said I did not, I would be a liar like you, but I do know him and obey his word. Your father Abraham rejoiced at the thought of seeing my day; he saw it and was glad." "You are not yet fifty years old," they said to him, "and you have seen Abraham!" "Very truly I tell you," Jesus answered, "before Abraham was born, I am!" At this, they picked up stones to stone him, but Jesus hid himself, slipping away from the temple grounds. (John 8:54-59)*

9. What does Jesus claim about himself in each of the following sections of John 8:28-59?

   - Vv. 28-29—

   - V. 42—

   - Vv. 43-47—

   - Vv. 54-59—

Jesus claims to speak what Father God has taught him and to always do what pleases God. And no man can prove him guilty of any sin. These are fantastic claims to make by anyone who was not absolutely certain that they are true. Jesus knew who he was. He knew his purpose.

> **Scriptural Insight:** When Jesus said, "Before Abraham was, I am," that "I am" was the name by which the Jews knew their God—in Hebrew, *Yahweh*. The listeners knew immediately that Jesus was claiming to be God himself. That infuriated them. But Jesus claimed it without hesitation regardless of the danger to himself. Regarding his innocence: Though Jesus was executed by Rome as a state criminal (the meaning of crucifixion), his innocence was repeatedly confirmed by others: Pontius Pilate (Luke 23:4,13-15,22), King Herod Antipas (Luke 23:8-12,15), a crucified criminal (Luke 23:41), and a Roman centurion (Luke 23:47).

10. What does Jesus claim about himself in John 17:5, 24?

Twice in this beautiful prayer of John 17, Jesus spoke about the relationship he had with his Father before he was sent to earth and even before the world was ever created. Together they had existed in relationship, and it was special to Jesus, a relationship of love between the Father and the Son. From this love relationship flows the love that Jesus has for all those who follow him.

11. Read Psalm 110:1. what position of authority would the promised Messiah (my Lord) hold?

12. Read Daniel 7:13-14 and Mark 14:61-64.

- According to Daniel's vision, how would the promised Messiah (my Lord) come to earth?

- What position of authority would the promised Messiah (son of man, v. 14) hold?

- In Mark 14, what did Jesus claim about himself regarding his being the promised Messiah?

Jesus claimed these truths for himself in the gospels. He called himself the Son of Man (seen often in Luke's gospel). During his trial, though he did not defend himself against accusations of wrongdoing, he did answer the questions related to his identity. Jesus said that he would be seen sitting at the right hand of God (Psalm 110:1) and coming on the clouds of heaven (Daniel 7:13-14). There is absolutely no doubt that Jesus claimed to be God and to have the authority of God.

The coming of Jesus Christ into human history was not an event that suddenly burst upon an unsuspecting world. It was the fulfillment of a long line of prophecies that started with the beginning of human history (Genesis 3:15). The arrival of Jesus in human form was planned before the creation of the world as well as the mission he was sent to accomplish—reconciling the world to God (2 Timothy 1:9; 1 Peter 1:20).

Our God is a God you can know

13. Read John 14:6-10. What does Jesus say about our being able to know God?

> **Focus on the Meaning:** The invisible God can be seen and known through His Son, Jesus Christ, who is both God and man.

A relationship with God must be based on a true knowledge of the God who is. The Bible teaches that humans can know truth about God. Jesus declared that one must go through him to know God the Father. Jesus also demonstrated that seeing and knowing him is the same as seeing and knowing God the Father. Both Jesus' words and his works come from God living in Jesus. The New Testament asserts that the invisible God can be known through his Son. Jesus is our Savior and our ultimate grace gift from God!

14. *Graceful Living:* Read Matthew 16:13-17. Notice the question Jesus asked his disciples. This is the world's most important question: "Who do you say Jesus is?" Many want to tell you that he was just a great religious teacher. But was he just that?

In his book *Mere Christianity*, the great 20th century thinker C. S. Lewis posed this solution:

> A man who was merely a man and said the sort of things Jesus said would not be a great moral teacher. He would either be a lunatic—on the level with a man who says he is a poached egg—or else he would be the Devil of Hell. You must make your choice. Either this man was, and is, the Son of God: or else a madman or something worse ...You can shut him up for a fool, you can spit at him and kill him as a demon; or you can fall at his feet and call him Lord and God. But let us not come up with any patronizing nonsense about his being a great human teacher. He has not left that open to us. He did not intend to. (C. S. Lewis, *Mere Christianity*, pages 54-55)

As we have seen in this lesson, Jesus Christ claimed equality with God. Either he was God, or he was not God. If he was not God, then he was a liar (knew he was not God but claimed it anyway) or a lunatic (thought he was God). Either way, you must decide. Who do you say that Jesus is?

Respond to God in prayer about what he has shown you today.

Day Four Study

What others claimed about Jesus

Many modern skeptics say that Jesus never claimed to be God and that the writers of the New Testament never claimed that he was God. It is important that we test these statements against what the New Testament writers did claim about the deity of Christ, based on what Jesus said about himself and demonstrated in his life.

15. Read the following passages to answer the question, "What claims do the New Testament writers make about Jesus?"

- John (one of the 12 Apostles) in John 1:1-3, 14—

- Peter (one of the 12 Apostles) in Acts 2:32-36—

- Peter in 2 Peter 1:16-18—

- Paul in 1 Corinthians 15:3-8—

- Paul in Philippians 2:5-11—

- Paul in Colossians 1:15-18; 2:9—

- The writer of Hebrews in Hebrews 1:1-4—

The New Testament writers are consistent in their claims about Jesus. They effectively declared that Jesus was truly God and not just a great teacher. If these writers knew that Jesus was not God and yet claimed that he was, you would conclude that they were liars, promoting a myth in order to somehow profit from it. But they did not do that. They declared what they had seen, heard, touched, and known to be absolutely true.

> **Historical Insight:** There were, to be sure, ways of coping with the death of a teacher, or even a leader. The picture of Socrates was available, in the wider world, as a model of unjust death nobly borne. The category of 'martyr' was available, within Judaism, for someone who stood up to pagans, and compromising no-better-than-pagans, and died still loyal to YHWH (the Hebrew name for God). The category of failed but still revered Messiah, however, did not exist. A Messiah who died at the hands of the pagans, instead of winning YHWH's battle against them, was a deceiver...Why then did people go on talking about Jesus of Nazareth, except as a remarkable but tragic memory? The obvious answer is the one given by all early Christians actually known to us (as opposed to those invented by modern mythographers). **Jesus was raised from the dead.... The resurrection, however we understand it, was the only reason why his life and words possessed any relevance two weeks, let alone two millennia, after his death.** (N.T. Wright, *Jesus and the Victory of God: Christian Origins and the Question of God, Volume 2*)

From the beginning, the church has maintained that Jesus Christ, crucified and risen from the dead, is Savior and Lord of heaven and earth. Apart from his resurrection from the dead, historians have no feasible theory for the birth and progress of the Church. Paul confirms what was being taught everywhere about Jesus: that he died for our sins, that he was buried, and that he was raised from the dead—all according to what was promised in the Scriptures. His resurrected body was seen by more than 500 people and on at least 6 occasions. There were plenty of eyewitnesses to these truths.

16. *Graceful Living:* Do you believe that Jesus was raised from the dead according to the eyewitnesses who claimed this truth? How does your faith about this truth influence your life?

> **Scriptural Insight:** The Christian church rests on the resurrection of its Founder. Without this fact, the church could never have been born, or if born, it would soon have died a natural death. The miracle of the resurrection and the existence of Christianity are so closely connected that they must stand or fall together. If Christ was raised from the dead, then all his other miracles are sure, and our faith is impregnable; if he was not raised, he died in vain, and our faith is vain. It was only his resurrection that made his death available for our atonement, justification, and salvation; without the resurrection, his death would be the grave of our hopes; we should be still unredeemed and under the power of our sins. A gospel of a dead Savior would be a contradiction and wretched delusion. (Philip Schaff, *History of the Christian Church, Volume 1*, page 172)

What does the Bible say about the "Trinity?"

While confirming that there is only one true God, believers have worshiped Jesus Christ and have spoken of him in terms appropriate only of deity from the earliest days of Christianity. The Holy Spirit is also known as deity. You may be confused how Jesus could be God and the Spirit could be God and the Father could be God. Who is the one that is really God? The answer is all of them: three-in-one.

The Bible clearly teaches three Divine Persons, each rightly called God, yet all the one and same God. The doctrine of the *Trinity* (or "Tri-unity," a man-made label) is a summary of the teachings of the Bible regarding the nature of God.

17. Read the following verses where the three representations of the one true God are mentioned together and fill in the blanks.

Matthew 28:18-20: *"...baptizing them in the name of the _____ and of the _____ and of the _____."*

---

2 Corinthians 13:14: *"May the grace of the _____, and the love of _____, and the fellowship of the _____ be with you all."*

---

1 Peter 1:1-2: *"...who have been chosen according to the foreknowledge of _____, through the sanctifying work of the _____, to be obedient to _____..."*

Luke 3:21-22: *"... _____ was baptized too. And as he was praying, heaven was opened and the _____ descended on him in bodily form like a dove. And a voice came from heaven: "You are _____, whom I love."*

The doctrine of the Trinity ("Tri-unity") was formulated by the church after many years of reflecting on the biblical data and after rejecting many inadequate theories. The "problem" answered by the doctrine was created by apparently contradictory assertions:

- Biblical monotheism - the insistence that there is only one true God. *Exodus 20:2-3; Isaiah 42:8; 45:5*

- That *without denying biblical monotheism,* the apostles and early church worshiped Jesus Christ and honored three Persons as God: the Father, the Son, and the Holy Spirit. *Matthew 28:18-20; 2 Corinthians 13:14*

- Therefore, outsiders accused the church of falling into either *polytheism* (belief in more than one God) or *idolatry* (improperly worshiping someone as God - in this case, Jesus).

Church leaders gathered in Nicaea (modern Turkey) to verbalize what God revealed about himself: one in essence, three in persons. They wrote what is known as the Nicene Creed.

> I believe in one God the Father Almighty, maker of heaven and earth, and of all things visible and invisible; and in one Lord Jesus Christ, the only-begotten Son of God, begotten of his Father before all worlds, God of God, Light of Light, very God of very God, begotten, not made, being of one substance with the Father, by whom all things were made; Who for us men and for our salvation came down from heaven and was incarnate by the Holy Spirit of the Virgin Mary...And I believe in the Holy Spirit the Lord and giver of life, who proceeds from the Father and the Son, who with the Father and the Son together is worshiped and glorified... (*Nicene Creed*, AD 325)

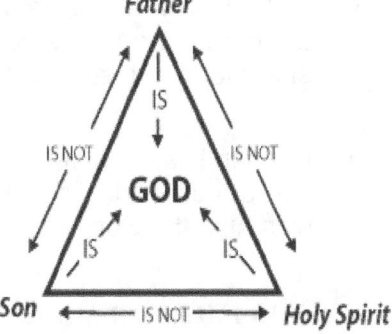

The doctrine of the Trinity was defined after careful Bible study and debate. Since the earliest century, it has stood as an accurate representation of the Bible's teaching: **God is one in essence, three in Person.** The diagram at right is an attempt to picture this.

18. ***Graceful Living:*** Read 1 Timothy 2:3-6. God invites all men into a personal relationship with himself through faith in his Son Jesus Christ. *If Jesus Christ is who he claimed to be, then knowing him is the single most important issue in all of life.*

- Are you confident that you have made the choice to put your faith in Jesus? If not, you can do so right now. Just tell God that you know you have sinned in his sight. Tell him that you are putting your trust in Jesus for your salvation. Accept God's gift of forgiveness for all of your sins. Thank him for his goodness to you and his gift of eternal life.

- If you are confident that you have already put your faith in Jesus, what choice(s) as a Christian have you made or do you need to make in order to grow in the process of knowing him?

> **Think About It:** Today, all sorts of subjects are eagerly pursued; but the knowledge of God is neglected...Yet to know God is man's chief end, and justifies his existence. Even if a hundred lives were ours, this one aim would be sufficient for them all. (John Calvin)

Respond to God about what he has shown you in this lesson.

Recommended: Listen to the podcast "Treasuring the Gift of Jesus Christ" after doing this lesson to reinforce what you have learned. Use the following listener guide.

Treasuring the Gift of Jesus Christ

CHRISTIANITY IS CHRIST

- Christianity is Christ! It is not a lifestyle. It is not rules of conduct. It is not a society of people who have joined together by the sprinkling or covering of water. Christianity is a relationship with the Lord Jesus Christ.

WHAT JESUS CLAIMED ABOUT HIMSELF

- Not only did Jesus claim to be God, but He also claimed to be the answer to the needs of the human heart. He consistently calls God His Father. He declared His right to judge and said that He deserves the honor that belongs to God.

- Even in His trials before the Jewish and Roman leaders, Jesus clearly and boldly claimed His identity as the promised anointed one of God. He claimed to be the Son of Man who was also the Son of God.

JESUS WAS FULLY HUMAN.

- Jesus was fully human. He experienced the normal process of body development from a child to an adult man. He obeyed His parents and learned to live with at least 4 brothers and 2 sisters. In His human body, Jesus felt hunger and thirst, tears and anger, distress and pain.

- Because Jesus was fully human, He understands every single one of your heartaches, physical pains, feelings of rejection, strained relationships, abuse, grief, and impatience. He gets your joy, too.

- Jesus was fully human, but He did not sin because He lived in perfect love for God the Father, His Father. Because He loved God perfectly, He lived in perfect dependence on God the Father and perfect obedience. And He gave us a pattern to follow so that we can learn to love God and to depend upon Him by faith, too.

JESUS WAS FULLY GOD.

- Jesus is the image of the invisible God. He is the exact representation of God's likeness. We are not talking about His face but His character. *Colossians 1:15; John 14:9*

- Jesus as the Son of God is the firstborn **over** all creation. This refers to Him being the one who had priority and supremacy over everything that God the Father owned. He inherited it all. *Colossians 1:15*

- Jesus was the Creator. He was not created. All things were created by Him and through Him. *Colossians 1:16; John 1:3*

- Jesus holds all things together. Christ is the controlling and unifying force in nature. *Colossians 1:17; Hebrews 1:3*

- Jesus is also Head of the Church. The Jews and Gentiles are combined into one body of believers, and He is the Head of that body. *Colossians 1:18*

- All God's fullness dwells in Jesus. The totality of God's powers and attributes are in Jesus. There is nothing missing. There is nothing more of God that we can get apart from Jesus. *Colossians 1:19*

- Jesus Christ is fully God and is Lord over all. Jesus not only claimed Psalm 110:1 for Himself but also demonstrated that He was the Son of God who sits at God's right hand. Jesus is the Christ. He is also the Lord. Lord means master.

- As fully God and fully man, you can be confident that Jesus as human understands how you feel and is powerful enough as God to take care of your every need. When you go to Him in prayer, you can trust that He understands, that He knows how you are feeling and what your needs are at that moment. You can trust His compassion toward you to meet your needs. Are you confident of that?

JESUS DEMONSTRATED HOW MUCH HE LOVED AND VALUED WOMEN.

- The Lord Jesus also demonstrated in His life on earth how much He loved and valued women. He taught them truth about God, forgave them for their sins, accepted them in His circle of followers, and gave new life to them after His resurrection. His care for them was so countercultural to what they had previously known. Women recognized that and responded with love for Him and a desire to serve him. Jesus Christ entered into the midst of their lives, visibly representing God to them, loving them dearly, and changing their lives forever! He does the same for you and me today.

- Jesus invites you to trust in what He says about Himself—that He is the Son of God—and believe that He died on the cross for you. Have you done that?

- As soon as you trust in Christ to be your Savior, you begin a loving relationship with the God of the universe. From then on, you have a new spiritual life with God's Spirit living inside you and producing many new qualities in you as you respond to Him.

- You receive complete love and acceptance by God as your Father. You receive treasure that is yours to know and experience for the rest of your earthly life. When you trust in Christ, He is in your life forever. You will never be without him. Ever.

- The treasure that God offers you in Jesus Christ is greater than anything you could substitute for Him. Why not spend the rest of your life getting to know this Jesus who gave Himself for you so you could have a new life? That is graceful living.

Let Jesus satisfy your heart with His grace so that your life overflows with His grace every day. You will experience a life of freedom and joy!

2: Grace-Covered Sin

The next day John saw Jesus coming toward him and said, "Look, the Lamb of God, who takes away the sin of the world!" (JOHN 1:29)

Ask the Lord Jesus to speak to you through His Word each day. Tell Him you are listening.

DAY ONE STUDY

Understanding the Gospel message

The ultimate grace gift came—Jesus Christ. But why did he come? What was his purpose?

From the time sin entered into the relationship of humans with their Creator God, the one question that continually demands an answer is, "How can I as a guilty, sinful human be made right in the eyes of a holy God?"

The spiritual problem of every person can be compared to death caused by a fatal disease: (1) Sin ("the disease" Romans 3:23) and (2) Death ("result of the disease" Romans 6:23). Our twofold problem demanded a twofold solution:

- For the problem of sin, people need forgiveness and righteousness. *Answer: Christ's* **death** *(the cross)*. We can now be cured of the disease.

- For the problem of death, people need regeneration (the restoration of life). *Answer: Christ's* **resurrection**. We can now be given life that is forever.

The Gospel message included the answer to both spiritual problems. The following quote by 20th century Bible teacher, Major Ian Thomas, captures the gospel message in a nutshell.

> Jesus Christ **laid down** his life **for** you...so that he could **give** his life **to** you...so that he could **live** his life **through** you. (Ian Thomas, *The Saving Life of Christ*)

This summary provides our subject outline for the next lessons. Lessons 2-4 examine what it means that Jesus Christ "laid down his life for you." Lesson 5 explains how he "gives his life to you." Lessons 6-11 will cover how Christ "lives his life through you."

God's holiness & human sickness

Our God is a holy God, meaning he is completely separated from anything that is sinful or evil. There is no sin in him at all. He is perfect. It is a unique part of his character—who he is.

> *This is the message we have heard from him and declare to you: God is light; in him there is no darkness at all. (1 John 1:5)*

Humans are not holy.

1. Read Jeremiah 17:9. What does the Old Testament prophet Jeremiah declare about the human heart (sickness)?

2. Read the following verses. What does the Bible declare about human sickness?

- Romans 1:18-23—

- Romans 3:9-12—

The desperately wicked and deceitful heart describes the sickness that is part of every human. Thus, there is an infinite gap between God's holiness and humanity's sinfulness. The Bible says (and you have no doubt seen this) that people willingly suppress the truth and exchange the truth about God for a lie. Such sickness leads to destructive behavior. And it leads to death and separation from a holy God. Not a pretty picture, but that is a reality we must all face.

3. What is God's pronouncement of judgment on human "sickness" in Genesis 3:19 and Romans 5:12?

Focus on the Meaning: The death mentioned in the verses you just read refers to physical death and spiritual separation from God after Adam and Eve because of sin. Both are the end result of sin's effect on all life.

4. Read Romans 1:18 and Ephesians 5:6.

- What do you learn about God's response to human sinfulness?

- To whom is God's wrath directed?

5. Read Mark 3:1-5. Jesus illustrated God's wrath toward sin. To whom is his wrath directed in v. 5 and why?

What is God's wrath?

When you read or hear about God's wrath, do you picture God raging with out-of-control anger? That is our experience with human anger so we might think that "his is the same, only bigger."

I thought that way for years. But several years ago, some good teaching helped me to understand that God's wrath is not a *mood* or a fit of *temper.* God's disposition toward sin and evil is as constant and unrelenting as his love and goodness. He hates and rejects evil in a perfect and holy anger. He will never bend or compromise with it. His own nature demands that he judge it through action. God's response to all evil and sin is righteous, holy wrath (Romans 1:18).

> **Focus on the Meaning:** Since God's first concern for his universe is its moral health, that is, its holiness, whatever is contrary to this is necessarily under his eternal displeasure. Wherever the holiness of God confronts unholiness, there is conflict: This conflict arises from the irreconcilable natures of holiness and sin. God's attitude and action in the conflict are his anger. **To preserve his creation God must destroy whatever would destroy it.** When he arises to put down destruction and save the world from irreparable moral collapse he is said to be angry. Every wrathful judgment of God ... has been a holy act of preservation. (A.W. Tozer, *The Knowledge of the Holy*, page 106)

Let's put this in everyday terms that you and I can understand. How much do you hate germs like the flu virus infiltrating your home? Do you use a disinfectant to clean with gusto and keep your family from getting sick? I don't know about you, but my disposition toward the flu virus or a stomach virus is wrath. It is pollution of my home. Another example is an ant infestation in your home. You do not invite them in and just ignore their presence while they take over your kitchen or bedroom, do you? I bet you do whatever you can to attack their presence and restore your home to a safe environment for your family. When I spray ant killer where I have seen ants crawling in my kitchen, I am expressing wrath against their destruction of my safe home environment.

God's wrath is far more serious, of course. Sin is much more awful with far more destructive consequences than the flu virus or ants. But you get the idea.

6.   Read John 3:36 and Romans 5:9. Who will experience God's wrath and who will not?

We will cover why being "saved from God's wrath" is true for believers in the next lesson.

7.   *Graceful Living:* Our culture tends to dismiss the seriousness of human sinfulness. We blame people and circumstances for our behavior and attitudes rather than our deceitful, desperately wicked hearts. Do you now understand God's wrath against all sinfulness, not just what others do that we don't like? Ask him to help you see human sin through his eyes.

Respond to God in prayer about what he has shown you today.

DAY TWO STUDY

Forgiveness of sin before Christ

Because God is holy, he takes action against sin. The Bible calls that "God's wrath." The word "wrath" in the New Testament translates a word that not only means anger but also punishment. God's love for his creation requires punishment for sin in order to destroy it. The punishment for sin is death.

But God's love for people and his mercy towards us led him to prescribe a substitute to take the punishment for human sin. Then, God could forgive the sin and once again have a relationship with people. This shows his desire to be in relationship with people. But something had to die.

8. What substitute paid the price for human sin in the following verses?

    • Genesis 3:21—

    • Exodus 12:3, 5-7, 12-13—

    • Leviticus 16:3-5—

> **Scriptural Insight:** Animals died to pay the penalty for human sin. The purposes of the animal sacrifices prescribed in the Old Testament were: (1) To teach the seriousness of sin. (2) To teach that God is forgiving, but that forgiveness comes *only at a price,* through the death of an innocent substitute. (3) To provide a place for a person to transfer her guilt & receive temporal forgiveness. (4) To point symbolically to Christ's ultimate sacrifice. The death of the animal was a sad and ugly thing just as sin is a sad and ugly thing. But the innocent animal's sacrifice provided forgiveness for human sin and opened the way for a person to have a relationship with a holy God.

9. The sacrifices prescribed in the Law given to Israel through Moses (Exodus through Deuteronomy, "the Mosaic Law") were a means for God to forgive human sin. But forgiveness under the Law had its limitations. Read Numbers 15:22-31.

    • What were the prescribed sacrifices to cover unintentional sin?

    • What if someone sins intentionally ("defiantly"), what happened then?

10. Read Hosea 6:6 and Micah 6:6-8. What does God say about his desire regarding a human heart?

11. Read Hebrews 10:1-4. Why was forgiveness through the Law ultimately inadequate?

From the verses in Hosea and Micah, it is clear that God wants obedience, not compliance. Compliance is an act of yielding to a wish, request or demand of someone in authority. It is basically just keeping the rules. Obedience is an act of submission to the authority springing from commitment and trust. God has always wanted obedient hearts more than compliance, which is just following the rules without the heart being touched.

Forgiveness for "minor" or "unintentional" sins was obtained through prescribed sacrifices. But for anyone who sinned defiantly (intentionally), there was no forgiveness through the Law. Those who deliberately sinned must throw themselves on the mercy of God. God measured the heart attitudes and responded to an individual's faith with forgiveness.

Therefore, people in Old Testament times received acceptance from God and eternal life in the same way as we do today—by **faith** in the merciful grace of God. For daily living, however, forgiveness of sin under the Mosaic Law could be obtained "up to date" but not given in advance. It was at best **temporary**.

God had a solution planned that would be so much better! We will look at this in more detail (and how it affects our lives today) when we get to Lesson 7.

12. *Graceful Living:* When Jesus was on earth teaching the Jewish people, he continually had to remind them about their greatest need. The Jews thought that their enemy was Rome and longed to be out from under the occupation. But their true enemy was their sin. The sacrificial system was not sufficient to get rid of human sin and change their hearts to be in tune with God and his purpose for their lives.

The same is true for us today. Often, we look at our situations or relationships as the enemy. If we could only fix this or that, we would be happy, less stressful and could pursue lives of purpose. Yet, our sinfulness would accompany us into the next situation or relationship.

Are you more likely to blame someone or something for your unhappiness or stress? Realize that trusting in Christ's sacrifice for your sin means that you not only get continual forgiveness but you also get power to deal with any aspect of life in a godly manner. Ask the Lord to help you realize this.

Respond to God about what you learned in today's study.

DAY THREE STUDY

The Cross: God's solution to the sin Issue

Jesus understood his purpose—to give his life for all humanity. This was no surprise to him or to God the Father who sent him. It was God's plan all along. Jesus knew he would accomplish his purpose through his death and resurrection.

13. What did Jesus teach about his purpose in Mark 8:31 and 10:45?

14. Read Luke 24:25-27, 44-47. What did Jesus say to remind his disciples about his purpose?

15. What did Peter emphasize about Jesus' death in 1 Peter 2:24 and 3:18?

16. What did Paul emphasize about Jesus' death in...?

- 1 Corinthians 15:3-4—

- Romans 5:6-8—

Think About It: Jesus bore our sins in his own body so that we might die to sin and live for righteousness. What a change in life strategy for us! And isn't God's act of love for ungodly humans while we were still enemies such an amazing thing?!

17. Read the following verses. Mark everything describing how Christ's offering is superior to the old Mosaic Law system. Then, answer the question that follows.

But when Christ came as high priest of the good things that are now already here, he went through the greater and more perfect tabernacle that is not made with human hands, that is to say, is not a part of this creation. He did not enter by means of the blood of goats and calves; but he entered the Most Holy Place once for all by his own blood, thus obtaining eternal redemption. The blood of goats and bulls and the ashes of a heifer sprinkled on those who are ceremonially unclean sanctify them so that they are outwardly clean. How much more, then, will the blood of Christ, who through the eternal Spirit offered himself unblemished to God, cleanse our consciences from acts that lead to death, so that we may serve the living God! For this reason Christ is the mediator of a new covenant, that those who are called may receive the promised eternal inheritance—now that he has died as a ransom to set them free from the sins committed under the first covenant. (Hebrews 9:11-15)

Day after day every priest stands and performs his religious duties; again and again he offers the same sacrifices, which can never take away sins. But when this priest [Jesus] had offered for all time one sacrifice for sins, he sat down at the right hand of God, and since that time he waits for his enemies to be made his footstool. For by one sacrifice he has made perfect forever those who are being made holy. (Hebrews 10:11-14)

When Jesus said, "It is finished" in John 19:30, he meant just that. Finished. Complete. Done once for all. What does the writer of Hebrews say to confirm that?

18. God the Father confirmed that Jesus' sacrifice on the cross was sufficient to do away with the old sacrificial system.

- What happened in Matthew 27:51?

- Before this, who alone could enter the Most Holy Place and with what (Hebrews 9:7)?

- Now, according to Hebrews 10:19-22, who can enter the Most Holy Place (God's presence) because of Jesus' blood?

- What is the benefit to us in doing so?

Scriptural Insight: God tore the curtain, for when the Lord Jesus Christ 'became sin for us,' and purchased our salvation by his own blood, the regulations of the old covenant were rendered null and void. Never again would God require the blood of a bull, a goat or a lamb. The priesthood was now defunct, the temple redundant and the law abolished. (Charles Price, *Alive in Christ,* page 80)

Whereas the gifts and sacrifices under the Old Testament law were not able to clear the conscience of the worshiper, the blood of Christ cleanses our consciences so we may freely and joyfully serve God. The sacrifices could never take away sins, only cover them. Christ's sacrifice, however, has not only taken away the sins but also made perfect forever those who are being made holy—all believers.

Now we can enter the Most Holy Place (God's presence) with confidence by the blood of Jesus. We no longer rely on a High Priest going in once a year to represent us before God. Jesus is our High Priest, his body is the torn curtain, and we can draw near to God with full assurance of already being cleansed of all sin. What a marvelous opportunity!

The human disease problem is cured. Christ has through his sacrifice done all that needs to be done to reconcile guilty people to a holy God. For any person, all that is required to benefit from what Jesus accomplished is to believe or trust in him.

19. Read 1 John 5:10-13. What can we know for sure, and why can we know this?

20. *Graceful Living:* We can know for sure that God has given us eternal life through faith (belief) in his Son. We have it already. Assurance of salvation can be known and experienced by (1) clearly understanding the gospel, and (2) trusting God's promises in Jesus Christ. Assurance is not confidence in our own ability to hold on to Christ but confidence in *him* and his promises to hold on to us!

- Did you know that you could have this assurance of your salvation?

- Now knowing this, how does it make you feel?

Respond to God about what you learned in today's study.

DAY FOUR STUDY

Justification by faith alone

Justification is God's act as Judge, where he declares a guilty sinner to be totally righteous on the basis of Christ's finished work on the cross and that person's faith in him. Justification involves both a negative and positive aspect. Negatively, justification is the removal of guilt from the offender ("forgiveness"). Positively, justification is the addition of righteousness to the one who believes (Romans 5:17). This is called the "Great Exchange." Paul describes it clearly in 2 Corinthians.

> *God made him who had no sin to be sin for us, so that in him we might become the righteousness of God. (2 Corinthians 5:21)*

Let's look at what the Bible says about this elsewhere.

21. Read Romans 3:19-28. This section is often called "the heart of the Bible." What is declared about the how and why of our justification (being declared not guilty)?

22. What does Romans 5:1-2 say about how we are justified before God?

23. What does Ephesians 2:8-9 teach about our salvation?

> **Think About It:** Do you want to give up the guilt? Or do you prefer to hang onto it like an heirloom? Forgetting you've been cleansed from past sins makes you nearsighted and blind and keeps you from developing maturity in Christ (2 Peter 1:9). A failure to recognize and trust that the sin issue between you and God is over will effectively stop your spiritual growth in Christ...We can become totally preoccupied with the thing that God is *finished* dealing with—sin—that we neglect what God is trying to do with us *today*—teach us about life! (Bob George, *Classic Christianity*, p. 60)

As Paul stated so clearly in Romans 3, we all are justified freely by his grace through the redemption that came by Jesus Christ. This comes to us by faith apart from any works that we do. This is true for all who believe (verse 22). It is a gift of God. He does this to exclude all boasting in our own efforts. We receive justification (being declared not guilty of sin) by faith in Jesus Christ alone. We will cover this more thoroughly in Lesson 4.

24. *Graceful Living:* Remember that grace is "unmerited favor." What are some of the benefits of knowing that not only is your salvation by faith alone but also your justification (your "not guilty" standing before God) is by faith alone rather than through any works you must do to earn God's forgiveness?

25. *Graceful Living:* Reflect on the words to the song below. You can search for it online to listen as well. Then, respond below.

Before the Throne of God Above

Old Irish hymn by Charities Lees Smith written in 1863 under the name "The Advocate"

Before the throne of God above
I have a strong and perfect plea (Hebrews 4:15-16)
A great high Priest whose Name is Love (Hebrews 4:14)
Whoever lives and pleads for me (Hebrews 7:25)
My name is graven on his hands (Isaiah 49:16)
My name is written on his heart
I know that while in heaven he stands
No tongue can bid me to depart (Romans 8:34)

When Satan tempts me to despair (Luke 22:31-32)
And tells me of the guilt within
Upward I look and see him there (Acts 7:55-56)
Who made an end to all my sin (Colossians 2:13-14)
Because the sinless Savior died
My sinful soul is counted free
For God the just is satisfied (Romans 3:25)
To look on him and pardon me (Romans 3:24-26)

Behold him there the risen Lamb (Revelation 5:6)
My perfect spotless righteousness (1 Corinthians 1:30; 1 Peter 1:18-19)
The great unchangeable I am (Hebrews 13:8; John 8:58)
The King of glory and of grace
One with himself I cannot die
My soul is purchased by his blood (Acts 20:28)
My life is hid with Christ on high (Colossians 3:3)
With Christ my Savior and my God! (Titus 2:13)

Respond in any way you choose (journaling, prayer, poem, art, song) to illustrate your thanks to God for ending the sacrificial system and completely forgiving you by your faith in Christ alone.

> **Recommended:** Listen to the podcast "God's Grace Makes Ugly Beautiful" after doing this lesson to reinforce what you have learned. Use the following listener guide.

God's Grace Makes Ugly Beautiful

Almost 2000 years ago, the beautiful Son of God voluntarily experienced the ugliness of sin and took on its punishment for our sakes.

SIN IS THE FATAL DISEASE.

- Our sinful spiritual condition is like "death caused by a fatal disease." Sin is "the disease," and everyone has it. It is fatal because the result of the sin disease is always death. Our sin separates us from having a relationship with our holy God. That is a spiritual death.

- But God's love for people and His mercy towards us led Him to take action. The Son of God came to earth to live as a human without sin and to offer Himself as a sacrifice for sin once for all. Never again would an animal need to die for human sin. Jesus Christ did that for us on the cross. Crucifixion was ugly. It was a place of agony and disgrace.

PSALM 22 PROPHESIED THE AGONY AND DISGRACE OF CRUCIFIXION

- Psalm 22 prophetically describes the agony that Jesus experienced during His crucifixion.

  - ✓ The crucified victim hung by his outstretched arms attached to the crossbeam. Usually heavy wrought-iron nails were driven through the wrists and the heel bones (Psalm 22:16).
  - ✓ As the victim hung dangling by the arms, the blood could no longer circulate to his vital organs, and he felt like he was suffocating. His bones would get out of joint (Psalm 22:14).
  - ✓ The victim would sweat profusely and be thirsty (Psalm 22:15).
  - ✓ Sometimes wood was nailed to the main post as a sort of seat. Only by supporting himself on this or by pushing against the nails in his feet could the victim lift himself up to gain any relief. Then exhaustion set in, and death followed, although sometimes not for several days.
  - ✓ To hasten death, the victim's legs were broken with a club so he could not keep pushing up to stay alive. The fact that Jesus' bones were not broken fulfilled another prophecy from Psalm 22.

- Psalm 22 prophetically describes the disgrace that Jesus experienced during His crucifixion.

  - ✓ The words in Psalm 22:6-8 describe the humiliation of public execution and match what the crowd actually said to Jesus.
  - ✓ The casting of lots seen in Psalm 22:18 was literally fulfilled.

WHY THE CROSS?

- Crucifixion provided the best scenario for Jews and non-Jews alike because both groups participated in the sinful act of executing God's Son. *Acts 2:23*

- It was God's plan for His Son to die on that cross for all of humanity's sin. No human being would ever come up with that plan. It requires faith alone, which is exactly what God wanted. *1 Corinthians 1:23-24*

As Paul persisted in preaching Jesus as the crucified Savior and sin-bearer, the unexpected happened: pagans, as well as Jews and God-fearers, believed the message and found their lives transformed by a new, liberating power, which broke the stranglehold of selfishness and vice and purified them from within. The message of Christ crucified had thus accomplished something which no [amount] of Greek philosophic teaching could have done for them. (F. F. Bruce, *Paul, the Apostle of the Heart Set Free,* p. 253)

- Every bit of our sin is so ugly to God. As ugly as the crucifixion. But our redemption is absolutely beautiful. God's in the business of making ugly beautiful.

THE BEAUTY OF WHAT CHRIST HAS DONE FOR YOU

- Because of Jesus' death on the cross, believers are cleansed of all sin and made new creations of life when God plants His Spirit within us. We are made alive as Christ is alive. That is beautiful. *Colossians 2:13-14*

- God gives us eternal spiritual life from the moment we believe, and we have complete acceptance before a holy God by faith alone. That which stood against us, the ugliness of our sin, is gone. Christ's life is given to us, living in us. That is beautiful.

- When we die, we now have hope of eternal life in the presence of God so physical death is no longer to be feared. Jesus frees us from the fear of death. *Hebrews 2:14-15*

LIVE OUT THE BEAUTIFUL.

- You get to live out this beautiful new life each day. Paul told us how to live this beautiful new life each and every day in Galatians 2 20:

    "I have been crucified with Christ and I no longer live, but Christ lives in me. The life I live in the body, I live by faith in the Son of God, who loved me and gave himself for me." (Gal. 2:20)

- The ugliness of the crucifixion becomes the beauty of Christ's life in you, in me. Are you grateful for the beauty that God has made out of your ugliness? Are you longing to worship Him for it?

- What ugliness in your life has God made beautiful because of Jesus Christ living in you? Let your heart sing out to Him joyfully today and every day. Graceful living starts with God making ugly beautiful in your life.

Let Jesus satisfy your heart with His grace so that your life overflows with His grace every day. You will experience a life of freedom and joy!

3: Grace Triumphant, Part 1

When you were dead in your sins and in the uncircumcision of your sinful nature, God made you alive with Christ. He forgave us all our sins, having canceled the written code, with its regulations, that was against us and that stood opposed to us; he took it away, nailing it to the cross. And having disarmed the powers and authorities, he made a public spectacle of them, triumphing over them by the cross. (COLOSSIANS 2:13-15)

Ask the Lord Jesus to speak to you through His Word each day. Tell Him you are listening.

DAY ONE STUDY

Christ's finished work on the cross

The gospel is an announcement to the world of an accomplished fact. What God set out to do for humans, he accomplished. The apostles declared this from the time of Pentecost (Acts 2) and beyond.

> *Therefore, my brothers, I want you to know that **through Jesus the forgiveness of sins is proclaimed** to you. Through him everyone who believes is justified from everything you could not be justified from by the Law of Moses. (Acts 13:38-39)*

Salvation is available on the basis of a single condition: faith (or "belief"). God acted; we are to respond to his action.

> *For God so loved the world, that he gave his one and only Son, that **whoever believes in him** shall not perish but have eternal life. (John 3:16)*

Those who respond with faith in Jesus Christ, God's Son, receive a firm assurance of eternal security (1 John 5:13), a secure new identity in Christ (2 Corinthians 5:17), and a true knowledge of God as seen through all that he has done through Christ's finished work on the cross.

Six terms describe how our relationship with God is changed because of our faith in Jesus Christ— Propitiation, Reconciliation, Redemption, Forgiveness, Justification, and Sanctification. These 6 relationship changes are the direct result of **Christ's finished work on the cross** so they have been called "words of the cross." They are in the Bible and part of your new identity in Christ. You need to know what they mean. ☺

The diagram at right shows these 6 "words of the cross." We will cover Propitiation, Reconciliation, and Redemption in this lesson. Lesson 4 will cover Forgiveness, Justification, and Sanctification.

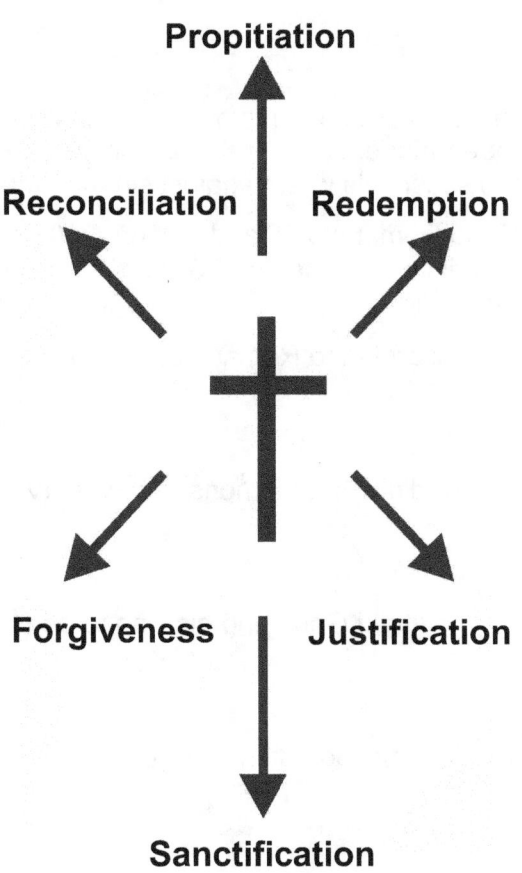

Word of the Cross #1 PROPITIATION: "God's holy wrath against our sin is fully satisfied"

It comes up time and time again. People who know Christ, having trusted in him for salvation and new life, struggle with the notion that God is still angry with them because of something they have done in the past. Maybe that is how you feel.

Do you wonder if you have a flawed understanding of salvation? Is salvation just getting eternal life when you die? From what are Christians saved? When you study the New Testament, you see that we are saved from many things—ourselves and our own flawed righteousness, for example. But we are particularly saved from the wrath of God. What does that mean? And how does understanding that give you confidence that God is no longer angry with you or at you?

Recall what you learned about the wrath of God in Lesson 2. Remember that God's wrath is not a mood or a fit of temper. It is his determination against sin and evil. God hates sin. It incurs his anger. Some kind of restitution is needed to "appease" his anger against sin. The Old Testament sacrifices temporarily appeased God's anger against sin. The word used to describe that is "propitiation."

Propitiation (pronounced like initiation) is an old word that basically means to satisfy or appease someone in order to win favor from them. That implies you have done something to lose their favor, usually something incurring anger.

1. Recall a time when you incurred the anger of someone you love and needed to make some kind of restitution to "appease" their anger. Or perhaps your anger was fully satisfied by restitution someone else made. If that happened, what was required? How did that feel?

The act of appeasement you just described led to someone now being satisfied because restitution has been made. So the relationship can be restored. That is what God did for us. He had a better plan to satisfy his wrath against sin than the animal sacrifices of the Mosaic Law.

2. Read Romans 3:25 and 1 John 4:10. Note: your translation may not read "propitiation," but "sacrifice of atonement" or "atoning sacrifice" instead. The concept of God's **satisfaction** is the same.

    *   According to Romans 3:25, God displayed Christ publicly as what?

    *   He did this to demonstrate what (v. 25)?

    *   What did God send his Son to be (1 John 4:10)?

    *   Why did God do this for us?

Scriptural Insight: The NIV text note on Romans 3:25 says the phrase "a sacrifice of atonement" could also be translated as "the one who would turn aside his wrath, taking away sin." (*NIV Study Bible*, page 1710)

3. Read Romans 5:9. What is the promise?

God took action. **God's holy wrath against all sin is fully satisfied by Jesus' sacrifice on the cross.** Because of what Jesus finished on the cross, God is able to extend mercy to every believer in Christ without compromise with evil. This is truth for you to know and claim.

Mercy is commonly defined as "not getting what we deserve." Our problem before Christ: God's righteous anger toward human sin. Without appeasement, all people are justly destined for eternal punishment. But God, out of his great mercy, provided a way for his anger against human sin to be satisfied through blood sacrifice on the Day of Atonement in the Old Testament (Leviticus 16) and finally through Jesus' sacrificial death on the cross.

Focus on the Meaning: In the New Testament, the word used to describe God's "satisfaction" with Jesus' shed blood (Gr., *hilasterion*) also describes the top surface of the Ark of the Covenant in the Holy of Holies, which was called the "atonement cover" or the "mercy seat" in Hebrews 9:5, depending on the translation. The mercy seat was sprinkled with the blood of the sacrificed animal on the annual Day of Atonement. By this ceremony, God's anger at sin was appeased, and the people's sins were forgiven up to that point.

4. From 1 John 2:2, to whom does God's offer of mercy extend?

5. From John 3:36, on whom does the wrath of God remain?

Think About It: Because Jesus Christ has endured in our place the full wrath of God for our sins, God is able to extend mercy without compromise with evil. His holiness **has been fully satisfied** with the offering of Jesus Christ. The payment has been made for the whole world. God's mercy extends to the whole world. But it must be individually acknowledged. God acted. The response he asks is belief in his Son. Why would anyone not jump at the opportunity to take this wonderful offer?!

God is satisfied...no longer angry at your sin.

There is no longer any sacrifice that anyone can ever do to appease God's wrath against sin apart from what Christ has already done. Picture an empty altar—never again used.

Jesus did the appeasement for you. It is done, finished! Because you have trusted Christ, you can dwell on the FACT that God is no longer angry at your sin—ever!

Dance! Shout for joy! Sing!

Never again let your mind or emotions convince you that God is still angry with you because of something you have done in the past.

Sometimes worship songs express truth so well that it can get implanted in our minds and completely engulf our hearts. The second verses of two beautiful songs we often sing in worship are like that. When I am tempted to think that God is angry with me, I let these beautifully penned words remind me of the truth. The words describing propitiation are in bold.

> In Christ alone, who took on flesh, fullness of God in helpless babe!
> This gift of love and righteousness scorned by the ones he came to save:
> **'Til on that cross as Jesus died, the wrath of God was satisfied –**
> **For every sin on him was laid;** here in the death of Christ I live. (*In Christ Alone*, Keith Getty & Stuart Townend)

> When Satan tempts me to despair, and tells me of the guilt within
> Upward I look and see him there who made an end to all my sin
> Because the sinless Savior died my sinful soul is counted free
> For **God the just is satisfied** to look on him and pardon me
> To look on him and pardon me (*Before the Throne of God Above*, Charitie Lees Smith)

6. *Graceful Living:* You can know and live with confidence that God is no longer angry at your sin because you believe in his Son. God is **SATISFIED...NO LONGER ANGRY** with you because of anything you have ever done. How does that make you feel?

Dependent Living: If God's holy wrath against you has been satisfied, and you live in the freedom of knowing his graceful love more than his wrath, how are you at being a grace-giver to those who have angered you? If you are holding onto anger toward someone and no restitution has been made, ask God to enable you to surrender the anger and rest in his love and peace. Trust him to do that in your life. You can be a grace-giver like God.

Respond to God about what he has shown you today.

Day Two Study

Word of the Cross #2 RECONCILIATION: "Our relationship with God is restored."

At some point in our lives, we will all experience a personal relationship that is broken. You can probably think of one such conflict right now.

Broken relationships cause pain and often leave us confused about how we can possibly fix them. Most people want to be reconciled so that the relationship can be restored in some fashion. How sad it is when a broken relationship continues to remain broken and is not reconciled. What joy we experience when we see a broken relationship repaired and healthy again. Reconciliation is certainly a reason for rejoicing!

But what does it take for reconciliation?

7. Define reconcile using a dictionary. What does it mean to reconcile, especially regarding human relationships?

8. Most of us are aware of personal relationships that have required reconciliation. Think about one such conflict. What were the circumstances? Describe the pain caused by the broken relationship. What was done to pursue reconciliation? How did it turn out?

The broken relationship restored

As Romans 3:23 describes, all people have sinned and fall short of the glory of God. Before Christ, our problem was a state of alienation (separation) from God because of sin. There was an impassable barrier between us. A broken relationship. Some kind of reconciliation needed to be done. We could not do it on our part—no matter how many good deeds we did. There was always that chasm created by sin between us and God—like a deep gorge with no way to get across.

BUT GOD did something about that! I love those two words in the Bible, "but God." Whenever it looks absolutely hopeless for us humans, God steps in and does the exact thing we need. The word reconcile means to re-establish friendship between two parties, to settle or resolve a dispute, and/or to bring acceptance. Wow! Did we need that!

9. According to John 3:16 and Romans 5:8, what was God's motive for reconciliation?

Think About It: Grace is unnecessary without an object. Humans are the target of God's grace gift. It is offered to all even though some refuse it.

10. Read the following verses. What did our God do for us according to these verses?

- Romans 5:10-11—

- 2 Corinthians 5:18-20—

- Colossians 1:19-22—

Scriptural Insight: When Adam & Eve sinned, not only was the harmony between God and humanity destroyed, but also disorder came into creation (Romans 8:19-22). So when Christ died on the cross, he made peace possible between God and mankind, and he restored in principle the harmony in the physical world, though the full realization of the latter will come only when Christ returns. (*NIV Study Bible*, note on Colossians 1:20, page 1814)

11. From 2 Corinthians 5:19, to whom does this reconciliation extend?

Think About It: Jesus Christ has fully paid our debt, removing the barrier between God and humans. God's "books" have been balanced since the debt has been paid. God stands eagerly welcoming anyone who will believe the good news and come home (repent, Luke 15:7-10).

God's love motivated him to repair the broken relationship with us. And his offer for reconciliation extends to the whole world, that is, to everyone who chooses to receive it by faith. Picture a bridge built across a deep gorge. Jesus became that bridge for you to have a relationship with God. By your faith in Jesus, your relationship with God is restored.

Relationship restored...no longer broken

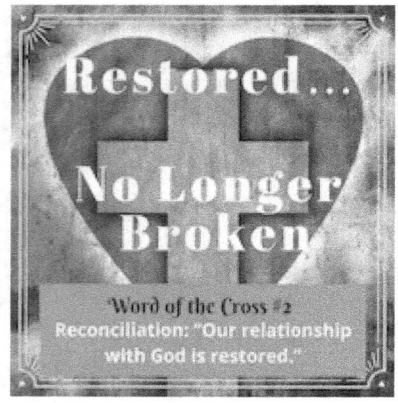

Because you have trusted Christ, you CAN KNOW and live with confidence that the barrier of sin has been taken away and a bridge has been built between you and God because of Jesus' finished work on the cross. It is done. Finished! This was God's act of reconciliation offered to you because of his love. All you needed to do was believe in his Son.

Your relationship with God is **RESTORED...NO LONGER BROKEN**. Reconciliation is a present reality for every Christian and is worthy of our rejoicing! Dance! Shout for joy! Sing!

Dwell on the FACT that your relationship with God is completely restored. It is no longer broken because of your sin. How does that make you feel? Are you willing to accept this truth and let it fill your heart with joy?

12. *Graceful Living*: Because of our restored relationship with our God, he has given us the ministry of reconciliation. We are to announce and appeal to others that they can have what we have in a restored relationship with the God who loves them. Look at your circle of influence (friends, family, co-workers, neighbors), consider ways you can be intentional in your outreach to them. Ask the Lord to help you make an intentional "connection" this week to spend time with one person who needs to know Jesus. Being intentional requires being strategic, deliberate, and planned.

13. *Graceful Living:* The same power of reconciliation is available to you through Christ for your relationships. If you are in the midst of a relationship that is broken and in need of reconciliation, ask the Lord to work his mighty hand in the relationship and provide you with his wisdom in pursuing reconciliation. What steps can you pursue to reconcile the relationship? Are you doing those in obedience to the Lord?

Dependent Living: Depend on the Master of Reconciliation to give you the wisdom and the strength to pursue reconciliation for a broken relationship. Trust Him to work in that relationship on your behalf. He is faithful and can do it.

Respond to God about what he has shown you today.

DAY THREE STUDY

Word of the Cross #3 REDEMPTION: "Purchased out of bondage to sin and released into freedom to serve God."

Bondage. No one likes being in bondage. Whether it is to a person, a contract, a debt, or something controlling your life, bondage stinks. It stifles. It discourages. It makes you a slave of whatever is holding you "in chains." I have been in one of those bondage situations. Perhaps you have been there, too. Every person who is in bondage longs to be released from those chains. Released.

Did you know that every human being born on this planet is born into bondage? It doesn't matter how much money or status you have. You were born into bondage. Bondage to what? Jesus called it being a "slave to sin" in John 8:34. And Romans 6:15-18 gives us a description of what that looks like. The slave master "sin" calls the shots. Obedience comes too easily. It is a trap. But you are released from that trap the moment you trust in Jesus Christ. The Bible calls this "redemption." We sing songs about being redeemed. But do we really understand what that means?

14. Look up the definition of redemption. Try to think of modern examples of redemption.

Did you think of the payment of a ransom for a kidnapped person? Another example of redemption might be the pawning of an item of value then going back later to pay what is owed on the "loan" to get that item back. Some energetic people like to buy "fixer upper" houses and flip them, turning each into a beautiful home. All those are examples of redemption.

Redemption in the New Testament is based on an understanding of the pain of slavery—a common practice in the Roman Empire at the time. Nearly 50% of the people were slaves—1 out of every 2 men, women, and children! The readers of the New Testament were very familiar with the hopelessness of being owned by a slave master as well as the buying and selling associated with the slave market. The only two ways out of the miserable cycle were to die or to be bought by someone who would set you free.

> **From the Greek:** The biblical doctrine of redemption is found in the combined
> meaning of four Greek words:
> *Agorázo* - the ordinary word, "to buy" or "to purchase." (1 Cor. 6:20)
> *Exagorazo* - "to buy out of the market"; i.e., to remove from further sale. (Gal. 3:13)
> *Lutroo* - "to loose by a price; to ransom." (Mark 10:45)
> *Apolútrosis* - "a loosing away." (Eph. 1:7)

Redemption represents an important change in our relationship with God. Before Christ, we were in a state of slavery to sin and to death (spiritual & physical). But God once again had a solution to this human misery.

Jesus came to set us free

15. Read Mark 10:45. What did Jesus declare about his purpose?

16. Read Ephesians 1:7. How are we redeemed?

17. From what did Jesus Christ redeem us and why?

- Galatians 3:13-14—

- Titus 2:13-14—

- 1 Peter 1:18-19—

Spiritual Insight: In the Bible, to redeem means to free someone from something bad by paying a penalty or a ransom (see Exodus 21:30; 13:13). Likewise, in the Greek world slaves could be redeemed by the payment of a price, either by someone else or by the slave himself. Similarly, Jesus redeems believers from the "curse of the law" (Gal. 3:13) and "all wickedness" (Titus 2:14). The ransom price is not silver or gold, but Christ's blood (Ephesians 1:7; 1 Peter 1:19; Rev. 5:9). (*NIV Study Bible,* note on 1 Peter 1:19, page 1889)

18. Read Colossians 1:13-14.
- From what have we been rescued?

- To what have we been brought?

Think About It: Since Jesus Christ has paid a full ransom price, the believer is a possession of God and is secure in freedom until his complete redemption (of the body) is accomplished.

19. According to Revelation 5:9-10, who has Jesus purchased with his blood and for what purpose?

Scriptural Insight: How far does redemption extend? Some of the biblical words describe a work *universal* in scope ("for the whole world," "the sovereign Lord who bought" the false teachers in 2 Peter 2:1), while others seem to be *particular* ("for believers" in Ephesians 1:7). While controversies occasionally erupt over which view represents the "true" one, the bottom line seems clear: The death of Jesus Christ is *fully sufficient for the whole world,* but it is only applied to those who put their trust in him.

20. Read the following verses. Using colored pens or pencils, mark everything related to being a slave to sin with one color and everything related to being a servant of God with another color. Then, contrast the life of slavery to sin from the life of freedom offered through your redemption.

    What then? Shall we sin because we are not under the law but under grace? By no means! Don't you know that when you offer yourselves to someone as obedient slaves, you are slaves of the one you obey—whether you are slaves to sin, which leads to death, or to obedience, which leads to righteousness? But thanks be to God that, though you used to be slaves to sin, you have come to obey from your heart the pattern of teaching that has now claimed your allegiance. You have been set free from sin and have become slaves to righteousness. I am using an example from everyday life because of your human limitations. Just as you used to offer yourselves as slaves to impurity and to ever-increasing wickedness, so now offer yourselves as slaves to righteousness leading to holiness. When you were slaves to sin, you were free from the control of righteousness. What benefit did you reap at that time from the things you are now ashamed of? Those things result in death! But now that you have been set free from sin and have become slaves of God, the benefit you reap leads to holiness, and the result is eternal life. For the wages of sin is death, but the gift of God is eternal life in Christ Jesus our Lord. (Romans 6:15-23)

    Slavery to sin leads to what results?   Serving God leads to what results?

Released...no longer in bondage

> Redeemed how I love to proclaim it. Redeemed by the blood of the Lamb. Redeemed through his infinite mercy, his child and forever I am. (Fannie Crosby)

God chooses to redeem us. It is an extension of his love and his purpose for us.

God redeems us to rescue us from the dominion of darkness and bring us into the kingdom of the Son he loves where we have forgiveness of sins.

God redeems us from all wickedness to purify for himself a people that are his very own, eager to do what is good.

God redeems men and women from every tribe, language, people, and nation to be a kingdom and priests to serve him.

When God redeems you, you become the possession of a loving, merciful God and can live in the security of your freedom from bondage to sin. And here is the best part. You have a new master now with greater power living inside of you—the Spirit of God himself—who can give you freedom from any entrapping sin. Claim that freedom now. Choose to obey the Spirit inside you who will lead you and empower you to say "no" to sin.

Dwell on the FACT that you, as a believer, have been purchased by the blood of Christ out of slavery to sin and released into freedom as God's act of redemption. You have been **RELEASED...NO LONGER IN BONDAGE** to sin. Dance! Shout! Sing!

The third verse *In Christ Alone* illustrates redemption this way (bold letters):

> There in the ground his body lay; light of the world by darkness slain:
> Then bursting forth in glorious Day; up from the grave he rose again!
> And as he stands in victory **sin's curse has lost its grip on me**,
> For I am his and he is mine - **bought with the precious blood of Christ.**

21. *Graceful Living:* You have been freed from a life of slavery to sin. Your freedom makes it possible for you to offer yourself to God and his righteousness instead. The rewards are holiness, lavished grace, eternal life, and a heart that is obedient to God.

    Are you experiencing the freedom from slavery to sin in your life right now? If not, do you have confidence that you do not have to listen to the voice of your old slave master sin?

    Reflect on this: You have a new master with greater power living inside of you, the Spirit of God himself, who can give you freedom from any entrapping sin. Claim that freedom now. Choose to obey the Spirit inside you who will lead you and empower you to say "no" to sin. That's dependent living.

Respond to God about what he has shown you today.

Day Four Study

An understanding of Christ's finished work on the cross is the basis for a firm knowledge of our identity in him—a foundational truth for successful Christian living. It was totally **God's work** to make sinners acceptable again in his sight. Our proper response is to **trust** and **rest in his work,** and to continually offer him thanks from grateful hearts along with our willing service.

Because of the cross, you can dwell on the FACT that God was fully **satisfied** by Jesus' finished work on the cross. God is no longer angry at your sin because you believe in his Son. You can dwell on the FACT that the barrier of sin has been taken away and complete **reconciliation** between you and God is possible because of Jesus' finished work on the cross. Your relationship with God is restored. You can dwell on the FACT that you, as a believer, have been purchased by the blood of Christ out of slavery and released into freedom as God's act of **redemption**. You have a new master with greater power living inside of you, the Spirit of God himself, who can give you freedom from any entrapping sin.

22. *Graceful Living:* In this lesson, you have learned about 3 words (Propitiation, Reconciliation and Redemption) that represent **Christ's finished work on the cross on your behalf.** These terms describe how our relationship with God is changed because of your faith in Jesus Christ. They also represent aspects of your new identity in Christ.

    The law of learning states that the best test of whether you have really learned anything or not is by explaining what you have learned to someone else. Review the meanings of these terms one at a time. Then, write how you would explain that concept (what the concept means for the believer, not necessarily the definition of the word) to someone who has not done this study but needs to know what she has in Christ. Think in terms of someone from a particular age group or stage of life.

    - PROPITIATION — How would you explain "propitiation" to a Christian who thinks God is always angry with them because of their mistakes?

    - RECONCILIATION—How would you explain "reconciliation" to a Christian who has been taught they have to go through a church official (alive or dead) to get close to God?

- REDEMPTION—How would you explain "redemption" to a Christian who is caught in a continual pattern of sin and feels like they cannot escape?

Respond to God about what he has shown you today.

Recommended: Listen to the podcast "The Gifts of the Cross, Part 1" after doing this lesson to reinforce what you have learned. Use the following listener guide.

The Gifts of the Cross, Part 1

As a direct result of Christ's finished work on the cross, our relationship with God is changed because of our faith in Jesus Christ. This change is described by six terms that are sometimes called the "words of the cross."

Each one of these 6 words answers a different question about our relationship with God. When you put them all together, you will never be the same once you see all that Jesus Christ has done for you. They are gifts of the cross for us.

WORD OF THE CROSS #1 IS PROPITIATION. IT MEANS THAT "GOD'S HOLY WRATH AGAINST SIN IS FULLY SATISFIED."

- God's wrath is His decision to preserve His creation by destroying whatever would destroy it—sin and evil. That's like you destroying viruses that invade your safe home environment.

- Our loving God took action. God presented Christ as a sacrifice of **propitiation** for our sins, a word that means to be appeased, to be satisfied. Therefore, God's holy wrath against all sin is fully satisfied by Jesus' sacrifice on the cross. Because of that, God is able to extend mercy to every believer in Christ. *Romans 3:25; Romans 5:9*

- When anyone puts their faith in Jesus Christ, they are saved from the wrath of God against sin. You get this by faith.

- Because you have trusted Christ and are now found in Christ, you can know and live with confidence that God is fully **satisfied…no longer angry** at your sin—ever!

- And that truth should motivate you to be a grace-giver to anyone who has angered you. You can be a grace-giver like God.

WORD OF THE CROSS #2 IS RECONCILIATION. IT MEANS THAT "OUR RELATIONSHIP WITH GOD IS RESTORED."

- All people have sinned and fall short of the glory of God. Before Christ came, we were alienated from God—having a broken relationship with our Creator. *Romans 3:23*

- But our God did something about that! God restored our broken relationship with Him by reconciling us to Himself through Jesus' death on the cross. It is complete reconciliation, never to be broken again. *Colossians 1:20-22*

- Because of His death on the cross, Jesus became the bridge for you to go directly to God, to be in His presence, not waving from afar.

- Because you have trusted Christ and are now found in Christ, you can know and live with confidence that your relationship with God is **restored…no longer broken** because of sin and guilt! Forever. God has taken away anything that separated you from Him—your sins, your failures, your mistakes. And God declares His arms open to you.

WORD OF THE CROSS #3 IS REDEMPTION. IT MEANS THAT YOU ARE "PURCHASED OUT OF BONDAGE TO SIN AND RELEASED INTO FREEDOM TO SERVE GOD."

- Every human born on this planet is born into bondage to the kingdom of darkness and sin as our slave master.

- If you know anything about slavery, there are only two ways out. Either die or be bought by someone who then sets you free.

- In Mark 10:45, Jesus declared that He came to give His life as a *ransom* for many—to pay the purchase price out of our slavery to sin with His blood. But more than that, we have been **released into freedom** to serve God with our bodies and souls in obedience to Hm.

- As an extension of His love and His purpose for us, God rescues us from the dominion of darkness and from all wickedness. He does this to release us to be purified as a people that are His very own, eager to do what is good, and to serve Him as His representative to others. *Colossians 1:13; Titus 2:14*

- He rescues us from this earthly body with sin still assaulting us and releases us at death when He gives us a new, perfect body, fashioned for life in heaven with God. *2 Corinthians 5:1-10*

- Redemption means you are the possession of a loving, merciful God and can live in the security of your freedom from bondage to sin because **a greater power than sin moves in**—the Holy Spirit. He **sets you free** from the power of that old slave master to become what God intended you to be.

- The moment you trusted in Christ as your Savior, you were set free from being a slave to sin in your life. God's Holy Spirit lives in you and makes it possible for you to say "no" to any sinful thoughts and behaviors. He gives you the freedom to serve God with your body, mind, tongue, eyes and hands. You are no longer a slave to sin. It has lost its grip on you. Turn to God's power within you to resist that old slave master calling on you.

- You can know and live with confidence that you have the freedom to live a life that pleases God in every way because you are now **released…no longer in bondage to sin.** Redemption is a gift of the cross we receive by faith in Christ.

All of these gifts are yours, dear believer! Because of Christ's finished work on the cross, you receive wonderful gifts by faith in Him. Propitiation, reconciliation, and redemption are treasures given by our loving God to us who believe.

Let Jesus satisfy your heart with His grace so that your life overflows with His grace every day. You will experience a life of freedom and joy!

4: Grace Triumphant, Part 2

But now the righteousness of God has been manifested apart from the law, although the Law and the Prophets bear witness to it—the righteousness of God through faith in Jesus Christ for all who believe. For there is no distinction: for all have sinned and fall short of the glory of God, and are justified by his grace as a gift, through the redemption that is in Christ Jesus, whom God put forward as a propitiation by his blood, to be received by faith… (ROMANS 3:21-25a, ESV)

Ask the Lord Jesus to speak to you through His Word each day. Tell Him you are listening.

DAY ONE STUDY

Christ's finished work on the cross

Salvation is available on the basis of a single condition: faith (or "belief"). God acted; we are to respond to his action. Those who respond with faith in Jesus Christ, God's Son, receive a firm assurance of eternal security (1 John 5:13), a secure new identity in Christ (2 Corinthians 5:17), and a true knowledge of God as seen through all that he has done for us.

Lesson 3 began our study of 6 "words of the cross"—the direct result of **Christ's finished work on the cross.** These 6 terms describe how our relationship with God has changed because of our faith in Jesus Christ.

The diagram at right shows these 6 "words of the cross." Here is a review of the first 3 terms and their meanings:

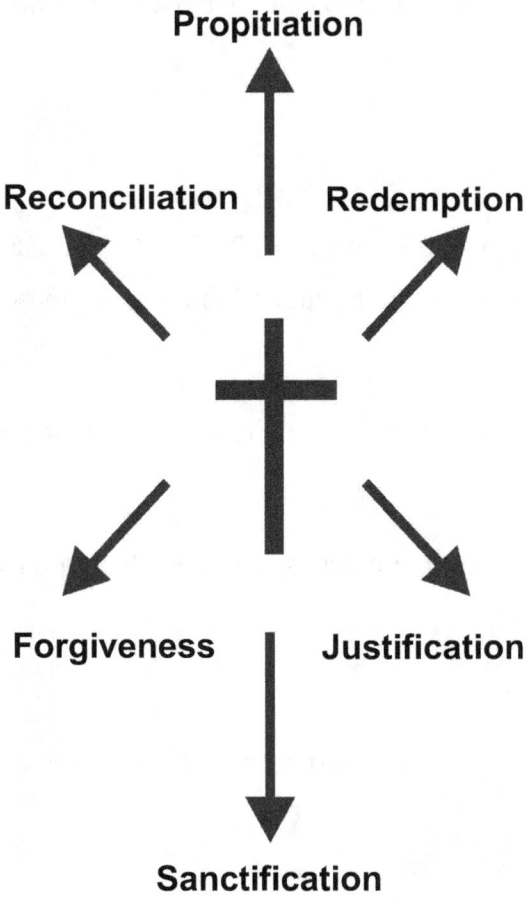

Propitiation

Reconciliation   **Redemption**

Forgiveness   **Justification**

Sanctification

- PROPITIATION: "God's holy wrath against sin is fully satisfied."

- RECONCILIATION: "Our relationship with God is restored."

- REDEMPTION: "Purchased out of bondage to sin and released into freedom to serve God."

Because of the cross, you can dwell on the FACT that God was fully satisfied by Jesus' finished work on the cross. God is no longer angry at the sin of those who believe in his Son.

You can dwell on the FACT that the barrier of sin has been taken away and complete reconciliation between you and God is possible because of Jesus' finished work on the cross.

You can dwell on the FACT that you, as a believer, have been purchased by the blood of Christ out of slavery to sin and released into freedom as God's act of redemption. You have a new master with greater power living inside of you, the Spirit of God, who can give you freedom from any entrapping sin.

In this lesson, we explore the blessings of Forgiveness, Justification, and Sanctification.

Word of the Cross #4 FORGIVENESS: "Guilt has been transferred to a substitute and taken away."

Like the woman washing Jesus' feet with her tears in Luke 7, many of us carry the guilt of our sins with us like a heavy burden, weighing us down. The continual reminder of our sins keeps us from experiencing freedom and from enjoying the relationship with God that we have by faith in Jesus Christ.

We don't just need a teacher. We need a Savior who comes in and does for us what we cannot do for ourselves: get forgiveness. All of our debt of sin before God is enormous; we are incapable of ever paying it back.

You and I need to understand how complete and continual is God's forgiveness of us. And we need to know how to deal with any recognized sin in our lives so that we will not continue to carry that burden of guilt.

What is forgiveness?

In the Bible, the term "forgiveness" means "to send off or send away." Our sin is transferred to a substitute, Jesus, and taken away. People in Old Testament times were accepted by God and received eternal life in the same way as we are today: by faith in the merciful grace of God. For daily living, however, they had to bring their animal sacrifice to the priest. Their sin was transferred to that sacrifice, and they received forgiveness for their sins up to that point.

God promised his people that one day forgiveness would no longer be a temporary solution, but be complete and permanent. Before Jesus came, all people were guilty before a holy God. God's answer is to take away the guilt. That happened on the cross through Jesus.

1. According to Hebrews 9:22, what was required for God to offer forgiveness?

2. Read Leviticus 16:8-10; 20-22 and John 1:29.

    *   What happened to the goat "for the Lord?"

    *   What was the role of the scapegoat (or, "goat of departure," "goat that escaped")?

    *   In John 1:29, what did John the Baptist publicly declare about Jesus?

3. What did God promise in Jeremiah 31:34 that he would do about people's sins one day?

Jesus Christ set you free from the burden

4. Read Colossians 2:13-14. What did God do to our sins for us? How many of our sins are covered by this action?

Once you place your faith in Jesus Christ, whatever you have done that was wrong in God's eyes from the time you were born through the time of your death has been canceled. Taken away. All of it. Past, present and future. Nailed to the cross. But it's even better than that…

5. Read 2 Corinthians 5:19.

- What do you learn about God counting our sins against us?

- What is the one sin that separates any man or woman from eternal life with God? See John 3:16-18.

6. Read 2 Corinthians 5:21. The action of God described in this verse is called the "Great Exchange." What is being exchanged?

7. According to Acts 3:19, what happens when someone repents of their sin (turns away from it) and turns to God?

8. According to Acts 13:38-39, to whom does God grant forgiveness?

9. Read Hebrews 10:19-22. What has God promised to do with your guilt as a result of Christ's offering?

Forgiven...no longer burdened

Make sure you understand this truth. God does not hold your sins against you. Instead, God places all of your sins on his Son Jesus. God places Jesus' righteousness on you in the place of your sins. That is the Great Exchange. What a marvelous act of grace on God's part!

We do not deserve this grace-gift. It is a gift of love. The only requirement to receive this gift of love is faith in Jesus Christ as Savior. You are forgiven based on your faith alone.

Only one sin separates any man or woman from eternal life with God—rejecting faith in Jesus Christ. What a relief that is!

Now, dwell on the FACT that you are forgiven and no longer burdened by your sin. Believe it and allow Jesus to cleanse your conscience from any residual guilt. Every time you think about it again, thank God for his amazing gift! Dance! Shout! Sing!

10. ***Graceful Living:*** Once you have trusted in Jesus, Ephesians 1:7 says that **forgiveness is something we possess as believers**. We receive God's forgiveness for all our sins (past, present, and future) from the moment we place our faith in Jesus Christ. That is very important for you to know. Forgiveness is complete and continual. Yet, many believers continue to live in guilt. Do you?

God promises to cleanse your conscience from guilt (Hebrews 10:19-22). Will you take him at his word? If there is any past sin for which you are still feeling guilty, claim God's complete forgiveness today. You can simply tell God,

> Thank You for forgiving me, thank You for cleansing me, thank You for redeeming my sin and turning something evil into something good. Thank You for being bigger than my sins, and being able to turn things around in ways I cannot imagine. With Jesus' help, I receive the assurance that You have forgiven me. Help my heart catch up with my head on this. Help me to see that You allowed me to go down that dark path into sin because You are able to redeem even the worst things we do. (Sue Bohlin, Probe Ministries, Sept. 2012)

I heard someone say that the "Today you" needs to forgive the "Yesterday you." Now, CHOOSE to believe you are forgiven and allow Jesus to cleanse your conscience from any residual guilt. Every time you think about it again, thank God for his amazing gift!

11. ***Graceful Living:*** Read Ephesians 4:32-5:1. Since you have been completely forgiven, what is Jesus now calling you to do in your relationships with others? Where is this the most challenging for you? Ask the Lord Jesus to enable you to forgive that person.

Respond to God about what he has shown you today.

DAY TWO STUDY

Word of the Cross #5 JUSTIFICATION: "The believer in Jesus Christ is declared righteous before God."

As a teen, I wrestled with the notion that I was not good enough to please God. I could never measure up to his standards of perfection. I was always guilty of not doing something right, of falling short of whatever it was he expected of me. Then, I heard some good news when I committed my life to Christ and chose to follow him—God declared me "not guilty" of all my sin. Not guilty? All my sin? Really?

Yes, dear believer, God declares you "not guilty" of all sin, once and for all, based on your faith alone in his Son. He does this even while you are still capable of sinning! It is an amazing plan that is totally based on his grace towards you, not anything you have earned by your own efforts. And this one decision made by God the Judge on behalf of every Christian is one of the most important aspects of our relationship with God. The word used to describe it is this: **Justification**. And the truth wrapped up in this one word has rocked the world for centuries.

What is justification?

Justification is a legal term that literally means, "to declare righteous, to declare not guilty." We introduced this in Lesson 2. English New Testaments use "justified" and "made righteous" interchangeably because they are translating the same Greek word. Justification represents an important change in our relationship with God. Our problem before Christ: our need for perfect acceptability before a holy God

12. Read the following verses. Mark every reference to justification / justified and righteous / righteousness. Then, answer the questions below.

Therefore no one will be declared righteous in God's sight by the works of the law; rather, through the law we become conscious of our sin. (Romans 3:20)

> *But now the righteousness of God has been manifested apart from the law, although the Law and the Prophets bear witness to it—the righteousness of God through faith in Jesus Christ for all who believe. For there is no distinction: for all have sinned and fall short of the glory of God, and are justified by his grace as a gift, through the redemption that is in Christ Jesus, whom God put forward as a propitiation by his blood, to be received by faith. This was to show God's righteousness, because in his divine forbearance he had passed over former sins. It was to show his righteousness at the present time, so that he might be just and the justifier of the one who has faith in Jesus. (Romans 3:21-26, ESV))*

- What is declared in Romans 3:20 about being righteous in God's sight?

- How does anyone receive righteousness (or be justified) according to Romans 3:21-26?

- Who gets to receive the "not guilty" verdict?

- God's justice demands punishment for sin. Based on what you have learned, how is his justice satisfied?

Scriptural Insight: God's forgiveness and justification of the believer are not due to compromise on God's part or a relaxing of his holy standards. These are possible because the sacrifice of Jesus Christ fully honored and *satisfied the righteous demands of a holy God.*

In our culture, we use the term "acquitted" for someone who is declared not guilty. And this acquittal is for the one wrong act of which the person is being accused. Yet, we do many other wrong things. For us as believers, God declares us "not guilty" of all sin, once and for all, based on our faith alone in his Son! What a deal!

Scriptural Insight: The term "justified" describes what happens when someone believes in Christ as his Savior: from the negative viewpoint, he [God] declares the person to be not guilty; from the positive viewpoint, he [God] declares him to be righteous. He cancels the guilt of the person's sin and credits righteousness to him...God will declare everyone who puts his trust in Jesus not guilty but righteous...Christ's righteousness (his obedience to God's law and his sacrificial death) will be credited to believers as their own. Paul uses the word 'credited' nine times in [Romans] chapter 4 alone. (*NIV Study Bible,* Romans 3:24 note, p. 1710)

Jesus Christ took your sin; God declares you righteous

God not only declares you "not guilty" of all sin through your faith in his Son, he also gives you a new status called "righteousness before God." Remember the "Great Exchange" declared in 2 Corinthians 5:21? Jesus gets our sin. We receive his righteousness. That is the end result of JUSTIFICATION: "The believer in Jesus Christ is declared righteous before God."

It is not your own righteousness that does it. You receive this righteous status by faith alone and not depending upon any works that you do to earn acceptability in God's sight, even after you are saved. When God looks on you, he sees his Son's righteousness taking the place of your sin—even your sin after you have been a believer for a long time.

Picture an accountant's spreadsheet dedicated to your life. On the left side of the page is the heading "your sins;" on the right side of the page is the heading "Christ's righteousness." When you and I sin (intentionally or unintentionally) for the rest of our lives, God replaces that sin on the "your sins" side with Christ's righteousness and puts your sin on his side—your sin is taken away (forgiveness). It is a continual balancing. Your sin never stays on your side of the page because God declares in 2 Corinthians 5:19 that he is "not counting men's sins against them." You are forever declared "not guilty" in his sight. Isn't that great news?!

But wait, there's more...

13. Read Romans 5:1-2. What do we get as a result of being justified?

14. If we were once enemies of God (Romans 5:10), what could peace with God (Romans 5:2) now mean? Add other verses that give you insight.

15. What does Paul declare about our change of relationship with God in Colossians 1:20-22?

> **Focus on the Meaning:** Justification is God's act as Judge, where he declares a guilty sinner to be totally righteous in his sight on the basis of Christ's finished work on the cross and that person's faith in him. Justification is by faith alone and not depending upon any works a believer can do to earn acceptability in God's sight. Justification involves both a negative and positive aspect. Negatively, justification is the removal of guilt from the offender ("forgiveness"). Positively, justification is the addition of righteousness to the one who believes (2 Corinthians 5:21).

16. Read Philippians 3:2-9. Paul describes his "confidence in the flesh" (including his efforts) to achieve righteousness before God.

   • What did Paul list to prove that he had reasons to put confidence in the flesh?

   • What did Paul conclude about his efforts in vv. 7-9?

   • What had Paul done to obtain his new righteous standing before God?

17. What does Paul declare about believers in Galatians 3:27?

Righteous...no longer guilty

Word of the Cross #5
Justification: "Declared righteous in God's eyes."

In Philippians 3:2-9, Paul considered his birth status, education, pursuit of knowledge, and zeal to get rid of Christians as evidence that he had plenty of reasons to convince himself that he was a "righteous" Jew and that God should have been pleased with his efforts.

But after knowing Christ, Paul declared all those things that he once thought were in his favor to be rubbish—a loss, not a win when it comes to faith. Instead, he discovered that knowing Jesus Christ as Lord was far better. He now preferred to be found in Christ with the righteousness that comes through faith, not by his own efforts.

All Paul had to do to gain his new righteous standing before God was to trust in Jesus Christ as his Savior and Lord. That is true for you as well.

You can dwell on the FACT that you have been declared righteous in God's eyes. You are now perfectly acceptable to a holy God based on your faith in his Son. How do you feel about this? Dance! Shout! Sing!

When you are tempted to think that God could not possibly accept you because of your weaknesses and guilty past, declare this to yourself: *"I am declared righteous in God's eyes because of my faith in Jesus Christ."*

18. ***Graceful Living:*** Are you still wrestling with the notion that you are not good enough to please God? Can anyone *ever* be good enough on her own merits to please God? No! Dwell on the FACT of your justification—being declared righteous so that you are now perfectly acceptable to a holy God based on your faith in his Son. How do you feel about this? When you are tempted to think that God could not possibly accept you because of your weaknesses and guilty past, what should you declare to yourself?

Respond to God about what he has shown you today.

DAY THREE STUDY

Word of the Cross #6 SANCTIFICATION: "Made holy for God's purpose."

I was once an up-tight perfectionist. Yes, I admit it. My whole self-image depended upon being perfect in grades, piano performance and whatever got me awards for achievement. Yet, my flaws kept getting in the way of getting straight A's one six weeks so that I missed out on the "straight A's" award for that school year. I was horrible in athletics so PE was my nemesis. Then, in college, physics knocked me down big time. I just could not see how to get the answers to those problems. My flaws were ever before me, and I sobbed when I could not achieve perfection—which happened a lot. My self-image was tied to a losing cause.

Then, Jesus entered my life and showed me a new way to look at myself—through what he did for me on the cross. When my eyes stopped looking at me and my flaws and started looking at him and my value in his sight, that burden of performance and perfectionism just rolled off my shoulders. It was the greatest relief I ever felt! And perfectionism has never controlled my life since then (although that tendency to evaluate myself and what I do with critical eyes remains latent in my personality).

Through my faith in Christ, God looks upon me as already perfect, as flawless as the most perfect diamond. The Bible calls this **Sanctification**.

What is sanctification?

Like propitiation (word #1), sanctification is a word we do not use in our daily vocabulary. To be sanctified means to be made holy. To be "holy" means to be "set apart for special use." The two words—*sanctified* and *holy*—translate the same Greek word so are used interchangeably in our English translations. They mean the same thing, though.

Sanctification represents another important change in our standing with God. Our problem before Christ: Our need to be separated **from** the world and separated **to** God.

19. According to Acts 26:17-18, believers in Jesus Christ have their eyes opened to turn from what and to what?

20. As stated in Hebrews 10:10, how are we made holy/sanctified in God's sight?

21. Read 1 Peter 1:16. What does God desire of us?

Sanctification is more than just having a different status before God. It provides a different purpose as well. Every believer has been set apart as God's special, beloved possession for his exclusive use. To be set apart for special use is similar to using fine china and silverware for special occasions. It is the opposite of ordinary and common. You are God's special, beloved possession—called by him to be dedicated to his service. How sweet is that!

You place your faith in Jesus; God declares you his saint.

Sanctified ones are called "holy people" and "saints" in the New Testament, depending on the translation. Whenever you see "saints," "holy ones" or "holy people," those words are translating the Greek word *hagios* (meaning "holy, morally blameless").

22. Who, in particular, are being called "holy people" (same as the word "saints") in Romans 1:7; 2 Corinthians 1:1; and Ephesians 1:1?

Focus on the Meaning: All believers are called "holy ones" based on their faith in Jesus Christ. You as a saint are identified by position, what God declares to be true about you. Every believer, including you, is one of God's saints, totally loved and accepted by him. You are considered a saint of God by his declaration, not because of your behavior. Although some particularly influential Christians have been titled "Saint" through the years as an honor for their service to God, this is no way negates the truth that **every believer is a saint in God's eyes**.

But wait, there's more...

Believers are made holy by Christ's death on the cross in their relational status before God. Believers are also "being made holy" in their thoughts, words, and actions by the work of the Holy Spirit. This is ongoing from the moment of salvation until the Lord comes or the believer dies when our "being made holy" is complete (Philippians 1:6).

23. Into what is the Holy Spirit transforming us according to these verses?

- Romans 8:29—

- 2 Corinthians 3:18—

Perfected...no longer flawed

An understanding of Christ's finished work on the cross is the basis for a firm knowledge of your identity in him—a foundational truth for successful Christian living.

Remember all those words we have already studied? You have been redeemed, reconciled to God, forgiven, justified and completely accepted by God because of what Jesus has already done for you on the cross. All of that contributes to God declaring you **holy** as one of his saints by faith in Jesus Christ. That is your status before God. **Perfected...no longer flawed** in his sight.

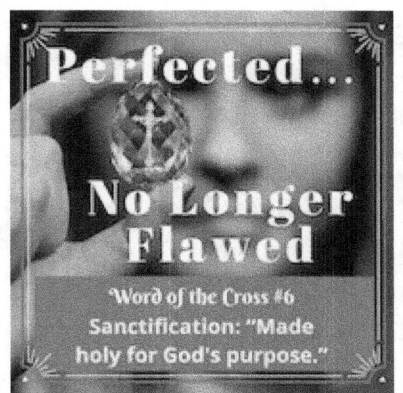

It was totally **God's work** to make you acceptable again in his sight. Your proper response is to **trust** and **yield to his work** and to continually offer him thanks from a grateful heart along with your willing service.

Dwell on the FACT that God declares you holy because of your faith in Christ. *You are set apart by him, for him.* This is your status before God because of your faith. You are made holy for God's purpose—perfected…no longer flawed in His sight. Dance! Shout! Sing!

Your behavior matches your position when you submit to the Spirit's work to intentionally separate you from what God calls sin and then commit yourself to being used for his purposes—24/7. You make that commitment throughout a typical day as you care for your household, be a parent or grandparent to children, work for an employer, interact with people around you, and spend your leisure time.

24. *Graceful Living:* Reflect on how you can commit yourself to God's use throughout a typical day as you care for your household, be a parent or grandparent to children, work for an employer, interact with people around you, spend your leisure time…

Respond to God about what he has shown you today.

DAY FOUR STUDY

An understanding of Christ's finished work on the cross is the basis for a firm knowledge of our identity in him—a foundational truth for successful Christian living. It was totally God's work to make sinners acceptable again in his sight. Our proper response is to trust and rest in his work, and to continually offer him thanks from grateful hearts along with our willing service.

Because of the cross, you can dwell on the FACT that God was fully **satisfied** by Jesus' finished work on the cross. God is no longer angry at your sin because you believe in his Son. You can dwell on the FACT that the barrier of sin has been taken away and complete **reconciliation** between you and God is possible because of Jesus' finished work on the cross. Your relationship with God is restored. You can dwell on the FACT that you, as a believer, have been purchased by the blood of Christ out of slavery and released into freedom as God's act of **redemption**. You have a new master with greater power living inside of you, the Spirit of God himself, who can give you freedom from any entrapping sin.

You can also dwell on the FACT that you are completely **forgiven** of your sins and that Jesus promises to cleanse your conscience from guilt. You can dwell on the FACT that you have been declared righteous (**justified**) and are now perfectly acceptable to a holy God based on your faith in his Son. And you can dwell on the FACT that God declares you holy because of your faith in Christ. You are **sanctified**—set apart by him, for him.

Humanity's disease was sin. Because of this disease, we were: 1) never able to make ourselves well, 2) in bondage to the disease, 3) alienated from the one who could heal us, 4) carrying the guilt of having the disease, 5) experiencing cumulative effects of the disease, and 6) unable to live a purposeful life. Jesus' finished work on the cross removed all these effects of the disease so that "by his wounds you have been healed" (1 Peter 2:24)—truly healed!

25. *Graceful Living:* In this lesson, you have learned about 3 more words (Forgiveness, Justification and Sanctification) that represent **Christ's finished work on the cross on your behalf.** These terms describe how our relationship with God is changed because of our faith in Jesus Christ. They also represent aspects of your new identity in Christ.

As you did in Lesson 3, review the meanings of these terms one at a time. Then, write how you would explain that concept (what the concept means for the believer, not necessarily the definition of the word) to someone who has not done this study but needs to know what she has in Christ. Think in terms of someone from a particular age group or stage of life.

- FORGIVENESS—How would you explain "forgiveness" to a Christian who is feeling guilty about their past?

- JUSTIFICATION—How would you explain "justification" to a Christian from a works-oriented religious background?

- SANCTIFICATION—How would you explain "sanctification" to a person who has trusted Christ after years of rebellion and immorality?

In a way—in spite of the power and importance of the six words of the cross—it can be said that they all have been accomplished to make the seventh great word possible: *"Regeneration,"* the restoration of spiritual life. This is the subject of Lesson 5.

Respond to God about what he has shown you today.

Recommended: Listen to the podcast "The Gifts of the Cross, Part 2" after doing this lesson to reinforce what you have learned. Use the following listener guide.

The Gifts of the Cross, Part 2

Jesus was fully human and was tempted in every way that we are tempted but without sin. Why is that? Here is the answer: Jesus lived in perfect love of God the Father. If you love God perfectly, you will never sin. Because He loved God perfectly, He lived in perfect dependence on God the Father. The result was perfect obedience to God the Father. Love for God leads you to greater dependency upon God, which results in grateful obedience to God as Jesus showed us.

Because of His great love for us—for you and for me, God sent His Son Jesus to die on the cross. From that comes propitiation. His anger against sin was satisfied. He is no longer angry at you, dear believer, because of your sin. From the cross, comes reconciliation. You can dwell on the fact that the barrier of sin has been taken away and your relationship with God is restored. From the cross comes redemption. You have been purchased out of bondage and released into freedom from any entrapping sin and to serve God in obedience.

WORD OF THE CROSS #4 IS FORGIVENESS. IT MEANS THAT "YOUR GUILT HAS BEEN TAKEN AWAY."

- Forgiveness addresses our guilt of sin before a holy God. God's answer is to take away the guilt. That happened on the cross when our guilt was transferred to Jesus Christ and taken away from us.

- Once you place your faith in Jesus Christ, the Bible says that whatever you have done that was wrong in God's eyes from the time you were born through the time of your death has been canceled. Taken away. All of it. Past, present and future. Nailed to the cross. *Colossians 2:13-14*

- But it is even better than that. 2 Corinthians chapter 5 says that God is no longer counting our sins against us. They all go on Jesus. Only one sin separates any man or woman from eternal life with God. That one sin is rejecting faith in Jesus Christ.

- Nowhere does Scripture teach that performing certain works (sometimes called "doing penance") or punishing yourself will make restitution for sin. This practice focuses on human works in order to be forgiven, not the blood of Jesus and our relationship with Him.

- Because you have trusted Christ and are now found in Christ, you can know and live with confidence that you have been **forgiven…no longer burdened** by your sin and guilt.

WORD OF THE CROSS #5 IS JUSTIFICATION. IT MEANS THAT "YOU ARE DECLARED RIGHTEOUS IN GOD'S EYES."

- Justification is a legal term that means, "to declare not guilty." Because of Christ's finished work on the cross, God chooses to give a "not guilty" status to anyone who places their faith in Jesus Christ. Not one human deserves this. It can never be earned. God gives this because Jesus paid the penalty for all sin.

- There are two aspects to justification. The first aspect is the removal of guilt from the offender. That is forgiveness. The second aspect is the addition of righteousness to the one who believes. That is justification. The two aspects together are called the "Great Exchange." *2 Corinthians 5:21*

- The amazing thing is that God does this while we are still capable of sinning! When God looks on you, He sees His Son's righteousness taking the place of your sin—even your sin after you have been a believer for a long time.

- When you are tempted to think that God could not possibly accept you because of your weaknesses and guilty past, declare this to yourself: "Because of my faith in Jesus Christ, I am declared **righteous...no longer guilty** in God's sight." That is a fact.

WORD OF THE CROSS #6 IS SANCTIFICATION. IT MEANS TO BE "SET APART AS GOD'S POSSESSION FOR HIS EXCLUSIVE USE."

- God, the ultimate perfectionist, determines what He considers good. None of our little checklists measure up. The only human who was ever good enough for God was Jesus.

- To be sanctified means to be made holy—to be "set apart from anything evil." By faith in Jesus Christ, God declares you holy in His sight.

- You have been set apart as God's special, beloved possession for His exclusive use.

- You are clothed with Christ (Galatians 3:27). When God looks on you and me, He sees Jesus and His righteousness, not all of our faults. His love chooses to do that for us.

- You are also "being made holy" in your thoughts, words, and actions by the work of the Holy Spirit. This is ongoing from the moment of salvation until the Lord comes or you die, when your "being made holy" is complete. We make choices that reflect our desire to set ourselves apart from sin and to God's purposes for us. *2 Corinthians 7:1*

- Because you have trusted in Christ and are now found in Him, you can know and live with confidence that you are set apart by God, for God. In His sight, you are **perfected...no longer flawed.**

All of these gifts are yours, dear believer! Because of Christ's finished work on the cross, you receive wonderful gifts by faith in Him. Forgiveness, justification, and sanctification are treasures given by our loving God to us who believe.

Let Jesus satisfy your heart with His grace so that your life overflows with His grace every day. You will experience a life of freedom and joy!

5: Grace-Given Life to You

But because of his great love for us, God, who is rich in mercy, made us alive with Christ even when we were dead in transgressions — it is by grace you have been saved. And God raised us up with Christ and seated us with him in the heavenly realms in Christ Jesus. (EPHESIANS 2:4-6)

Ask the Lord Jesus to speak to you through His Word each day. Tell Him you are listening.

DAY ONE STUDY

The Resurrection: God's solution to the life & death issue

You learned in Lesson 2 that from the time sin entered into our relationship with our Creator God, we had a spiritual problem that can be compared to death caused by a fatal disease: (1) Sin ("the disease" Romans 3:23) and (2) Death ("result of the disease" Romans 6:23). Our twofold problem demanded a twofold solution:

- For the problem of sin, we need forgiveness and righteousness. *Answer: Christ's **death** (the cross).* We can now be cured of the disease.

- For the problem of death, we need regeneration (the restoration of **life**). *Answer: Christ's **resurrection**.* We can now be given life that is forever.

The Gospel message included the answer to both spiritual problems and is simply illustrated by this statement:

> Jesus Christ laid down his life for you so that he could give his life to you so that he could live his life through you. (Ian Thomas, *The Saving Life of Christ*)

That is the gospel!

Doesn't that sound wonderful? But what does that look like? And why aren't all Christians enjoying this kind of life?

Many Christians have a lack of understanding of two **vital** truths:

> (1) Christ's finished work on the cross to secure our complete acceptance before God, and

> (2) "Christ in you" as the dynamic of daily Christian living.

As a result, believers may have a fairly solid understanding of God's grace as it relates to their initial salvation experience but an inconsistent, wavering understanding of God's grace in their ongoing life as a Christian. Many Christians also have very little understanding of the significance of receiving the very life of God through the Holy Spirit. As a result of such misunderstanding, Christians are often overwhelmed by failure, discouragement, and despair resulting from attempts to be perfected "by human effort." This may have been your experience before starting this *Graceful Living* study.

In Lessons 3 and 4, you got to see in detail the results of Christ's finished work on the cross. It is done. You are completely accepted before God. No more need to feel insecure about that. Those 6 relationship-with-God-changers—propitiation, reconciliation, redemption, forgiveness, justification and sanctification—are all true about you from the moment you placed your faith in Christ.

You may now have a fairly solid understanding of God's grace as it relates to your initial salvation experience. Your sins are forgiven, and you are going to heaven when you die. But if that is all you know, you will have an incomplete understanding of God's grace toward you for living out your daily life. And you might have little knowledge of the Holy Spirit's role in your ongoing life as a Christian.

1. Read Ephesians 2:4-6. Because of his great love for you, what has God done for you?

In Lessons 5 and 6, we will focus on the very life of God given to us by Christ himself as our **power for daily Christian living**. Through this life, we experience freedom and joy!

> **Historical Insight:** The great difference between present-day Christianity and that of which we read in these letters [New Testament epistles] is that to us it is primarily a performance; to them it was a real experience. We are apt to reduce the Christian religion to a code or, at best, a rule of heart and life. To these men [and women], it is quite plainly the invasion of their lives by a new quality of life altogether. They do not hesitate to describe this as Christ living in them. (J.B. Phillips, Introduction to *Letters to Young Churches*)

Humans as God created us to be

When God created man and woman in his own image (Genesis 1:27), they were created with a body, a soul (conscious life made up of mind, emotions and will), and a spirit that enables every man and woman to relate to God.

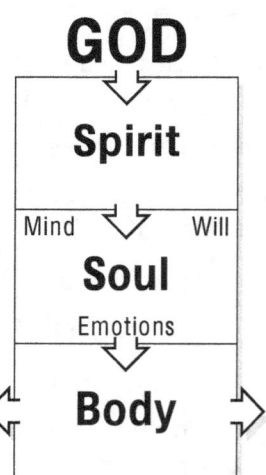

Our human spirit is the source of our inner drives for love and acceptance, a sense of identity, and for meaning & purpose in life. The human spirit was created to be a container for God's Spirit and was the means through which both man and woman enjoyed perfect fellowship with God. God works from the inside out. Adam and Eve were created to walk in a **dependent** love relationship with their Creator and, through that relationship, *bear the image of God* as the visible representation of the invisible God.

> **Focus on the Meaning:** Is man a "trichotomy" (made up of three parts: body, soul and spirit) or a "dichotomy" (made up of two parts: body—the seen—and soul/spirit—the unseen)? The best answer seems to be "it depends": *Structurally,* man is a dichotomy; *Functionally,* he is a trichotomy (the spirit of man being either inhabited by God or empty).

Through free choice (Genesis 2:16-18; 3:1-7), Adam and Eve forfeited their perfect relationship with God and introduced sin and death into the creation. Adam died *physically* 930 years later (Genesis 5:5). They experienced separation in their relationship with God. In the Bible, "death" means *separation*. Although they still believed in God and are in heaven today, Adam and Eve lost the life of God within them. And every descendant (except for Jesus) has been born spiritually separated from God and destined for physical death.

God, in His grace, covered their sin through an animal sacrifice, taking the skins to clothe their nakedness and guilt. This restored their faith relationship with God (see Genesis 4:1, 25). Because of their sinful nature, he could no longer dwell in them.

Natural man (in Adam)

2. According to Romans 5:12, 18, what are the effects of Adam's sin on every one of his descendants, including you?

3. Read Ephesians 2:1-3. What are the effects of Adam's sin on every one of his descendants, including you, before you trusted in Christ?

You might be wondering why God held Adam responsible for the sinfulness of the whole human race when it was really Eve who sinned first. A possible explanation is that Adam was created first. He became the head of the human family. He was the person in authority over and therefore responsible for Eve (Genesis 2:18-23; 1 Corinthians 11:3). The result is that everyone born into this world is considered to be born "in Adam"—i.e., out of his family line. The Bible often refers to this condition as "natural man." Therefore, since that day in the garden, all men and women are born without God's life within them, are sinners by nature, and are destined for physical death.

As a 20th century Christian author put it,

> We may not understand how we can inherit evil from our fathers, but there is no argument with the fact that as soon as we are big enough to sin, we go directly into the business of sinning. (A. W. Tozer, **Tozer Speaks: Volume One**)

Anyone who has been around small children knows for a fact that this is true!

All men and women are also born spiritually wanting, seeking to fulfill their purpose. Some have described it as having a God-shaped hole or vacuum in the heart of every person which cannot be filled by any created thing, but only by our Creator God. It drives our search for significance and our need for something outside of ourselves.

The diagram at right is a rough illustration of this "vacuum" or emptiness. Every human seeks to fill this emptiness with something that gives them meaning and purpose in life. As Paul wrote in Ephesians 2:1-3, we were "gratifying the cravings of our sinful nature and following its desires and thoughts." That is not a pretty picture, is it?

Regardless of your age or stage of life, circumstances or personality, you were created with a built-in spiritual hunger that only God can satisfy. This spiritual hunger and thirst are as real as physical hunger and thirst. The way to have it satisfied is just as real though not always obvious. How we do that determines whether that emptiness is ever filled.

4. Read the following verses. Using colored pens or pencils, mark what the believer has and can do with one color. Mark what the unbeliever does not have and cannot do with a different color. Answer the questions below.

However, as it is written: "What no eye has seen, what no ear has heard, and what no human mind has conceived"— the things God has prepared for those who love him—these are the things God has revealed to us by his Spirit. The Spirit searches all things, even the deep things of God. For who knows a person's thoughts except their own spirit within them? In the same way no one knows the thoughts of God except the Spirit of God. What we have received is not the spirit of the world, but the Spirit who is from God, so that we may understand what God has freely given us. This is what we speak, not in words taught us by human wisdom but in words taught by the Spirit, explaining spiritual realities with Spirit-taught words. (1 Corinthians 2:9-13)

The person without the Spirit does not accept the things that come from the Spirit of God but considers them foolishness, and cannot understand them because they are discerned only through the Spirit. The person with the Spirit makes judgments about all things, but such a person is not subject to merely human judgments, for, "Who has known the mind of the Lord so as to instruct him?" But we have the mind of Christ. (1 Corinthians 2:14-16)

The god of this age has blinded the minds of unbelievers, so that they cannot see the light of the gospel of the glory of Christ, who is the image of God. (2 Corinthians 4:4)

- What is true about the person who has the Spirit of God?

- What is true about the person who does not have the Spirit of God?

- What hindrances to one's understanding does the unbeliever have?

The terms "natural person" or "earthly person" used in the New Testament translations refer to any unsaved man or woman. As Paul described in 1 Corinthians, the unsaved person does not understand or accept the things that come from the Spirit of God. Their minds are even blinded by Satan so they cannot see the light of the gospel. Satan is the unseen power behind all unbelief and ungodliness. Every saved person is taught by the Spirit within us who reveals to us God's secret wisdom, the deep things of God, so that we may understand what God has prepared for those who love him and has freely given to us. Know God, know life. But no God, no life.

Think About It: The unbeliever is already: (1) alienated from God, (2) under the wrath of God, and (3) spiritually dead to God. Their problem is not just that they are sinners in need of forgiveness. **They are dead and in need of life!** When we become Christians at a young age or forget what it was like to live as a nonbeliever before Christ came into our lives, we can be very harsh on those who are living without Christ in this world. We expect nonbelievers to think like we do. Considering how God describes the nonbeliever in his Word, shouldn't their blindness and lack of understanding generate compassion in us rather than condemnation?

5. *Graceful Living:* If you became a Christian as a teen or adult,

- Considering the description of the unbeliever you just read, what was life like for you before you experienced Christ's redemption? What did you seek to fill your "God-shaped vacuum" before you put your faith in Christ?

- What drew you to Christ?

Respond to God about what he's shown you today.

Day Two Study

Jesus Christ – the Second Adam

Although he was God from all eternity, the Son of God took on a human nature and flesh, totally identifying with us in our humanity. Through his virgin birth, Jesus Christ entered the world spiritually alive and without sin (John 8:46; Hebrews 4:15; 2 Corinthians 5:21). He was the first complete man, from God's point of view, to live on earth since the Fall. Thus, he is the Second Adam (1 Corinthians 15:47).

6. Read 1 Corinthians 15:45-49. Compare the first Adam and the second Adam.

First Adam _____ Second Adam (last Adam) _____

7. According to John 1:14 and Philippians 2:5-8, what did Jesus (the Word) do to identify with humanity?

8. Read Hebrews 2:14-18. Why did Jesus need to be made like us?

9. Read John 5:15-19, 30. What did Jesus declare about the work that he does and what he seeks to do?

10. Read John 12:44-46, 49-50. When someone looks at him or hears him speak, what are they seeing / hearing?

11. According to John 14:8-11, what does he say about his words and works?

In his humanity, Jesus demonstrated for us the way we should live in dependence on God. He was doing the work of God (showing compassion, teaching, and showing kindness) and seeking to please God (not himself) with his life. He demonstrated to anyone watching or listening what it was like to live the kind of life that God designed us to do. He declared himself to be the visible representation of the invisible God, showing us the true way to God. Jesus completely identified with us in our humanity, sin (temptation) and death, so that we could be totally identified with him in his resurrected humanity, righteousness **and life** (Isaiah 53:6; Romans 6:4).

God provided a cure for our sin disease through Christ's finished work on the cross, BUT we were still dead and in need of life! We will cover God's solution for that in Day Three.

12. *Graceful Living:* If Jesus lived as a man dependent on God, how much more should we recognize our need to do the same? Read the "Dependent Living" information then answer the questions below.

> **Dependent Living:** In the midst of our messy lives, God wants us to learn to rely on Him more than on ourselves (2 Corinthians 1:9). If you have been reared in western culture, this is contrary to what you have been taught most of your life. To compensate for poor teaching in the past, women are taught from girlhood to "stand on your own two feet" and "you don't need anyone to be successful." So what does this relying on God look like?
>
> Are we as Christians supposed to stay like babies not doing anything for ourselves? Does it mean we are supposed to just lie back and let anything happen to us? Does it mean we are not supposed to use our skills, talents, advantages, and opportunities to be the best we can be? No! That is not what it means.
>
> We are supposed to grow and mature in our thinking and behavior. God wants us to give to Him all the skills, talents, advantages, and opportunities and use them for His glory. That involves following His leading and guidance. It means submitting our strengths and our weaknesses to Him for His purposes in our lives.
>
> Here is the key: Human parents raise their children to be less dependent on them and more independent. **But God raises His children to be *less independent* and *more dependent on Him*. Whatever He brings into our lives that makes us more dependent upon Him is good for us.** Dependent living is not weakness. It is being stronger and having more influence, success, and satisfaction than we could ever have through our own efforts—as brilliant and self-sufficient as we think we are or as weak and messed up as we think we are and everywhere in-between.

- Consider the areas of your life where you tend to live in self-sufficiency. Generally, it is in your areas of strength—your skills and abilities.

- The danger you and I face is getting too confident in our own abilities so that we do not rely on God in those areas we identify. When you recognize that you are acting through your own strengths and abilities rather than relying on the power of God, stop. Give your strengths as well as your weaknesses to the Lord Jesus. Ask him to work through those same strengths and abilities as you yield to his way of doing it. Pray about this today.

Respond to God about what he's shown you today.

DAY THREE STUDY

Regeneration: The restoration of life is God's solution to our state of spiritual death

The English word "regeneration" [Gr. *palingenesia*, from *palin* (again) and *genesis* (birth)] means simply a new birth, a new beginning, a new order. Regeneration is often used to denote the restoration of a thing to its pristine state, its renovation, as in the restoration of a piece of furniture or a car.

In the New Testament, regeneration refers to the giving of **life** after death.

13. According to John 10:10, why did Jesus come?

14. Salvation is described as receiving "life."

- How does Jesus illustrate this in John 3:3-6?

- What does Jesus say about this in John 5:24?

- What is revealed about this in Ephesians 2:4-5?

- As a result of being "born again," what is now true of us according to 2 Corinthians 5:17?

15. In John 14:16-17, how does Jesus give "life" to us?

16. How do Paul's words in Romans 8:9-10 confirm what Jesus said about how we receive "life?"

17. What do Galatians 2:20 and Colossians 1:27 say about our new life?

The restoration of life is God's solution to humanity's state of spiritual death. The Spirit of God enters the human spirit and brings eternal life with him. Jesus promised that God would give the Holy Spirit to us to be with us and in us forever. Forever! It is the Holy Spirit who makes our spirits alive again through his presence.

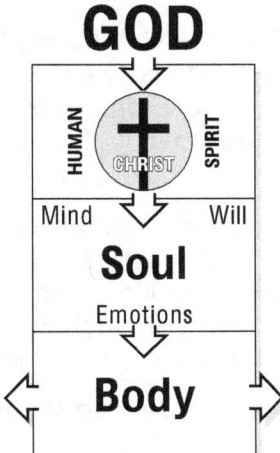

As the Holy Spirit indwells us, he unites (fuses) us to Christ. We get this from Romans 6:5 which says, *"For if we have been **united** with him in a death like his, we will certainly also be **united** with him in a resurrection like his."*

Resurrection brings life. And this life of Christ is in you, dear believer. Paul describes this as Christ living in you, "Christ in you." God fills our spirits with himself (see diagram at right). We, who were once dead, are made alive by the indwelling Holy Spirit who unites you to Christ so that "Christ in you" is a fact of your new existence. It happens at the moment of salvation (Romans 8:9) and lasts forever.

18. According to John 15:4-5 and Galatians 2:20, how should a new creation in Christ live? [Note: to remain/abide means "to dwell."]

God has access through your spirit into your soul (teaching your mind, guiding your emotions, directing your will) and, thereby, influencing your behavior. With the restoration of life begins a new adventure of learning how to live while abiding in Christ (making your home with him) and living dependently upon him to do anything of value. You are to live by faith; faith leads to dependency upon God. That is what Jesus demonstrated for us in his own life.

Consider how a caterpillar transforms into a butterfly. Something totally changes. The butterfly does not look anything like the caterpillar that preceded it. In the same way, you are not just a "forgiven caterpillar." You have been transformed into a "butterfly." Your greatest daily need is, first, to grasp the freedom of God's acceptance through Christ And second, to learn how to present your humanity to the indwelling Christ and experience true and abundant life.

Salvation is not just receiving something we did not have before (i.e., forgiveness of sins). It is **becoming someone we were not** before!

> Jesus Christ **laid down** his life **for** you so that he could **give** his life **to** you so that he could **live** his life **through** you.

19. Read Romans 6:11-14. What now should be our relationship to sin and the old life we once lived?

Because God shows his grace to us and forgives us of all sin, that does not give us a "license to sin" because we know we will be forgiven. A proper emphasis on Christ's finished work on the cross does not promote sin for a simple reason—in forgiving us, **God did not leave us as we were.** God transforms our hearts through the regeneration of the Holy Spirit. We who believe have God's law written on our hearts (Hebrews 8:10).

So when it comes to our old way of approaching life (listening to sin barking orders to us), we are to push back, say no, and not even present our bodies to sin to do its work. Instead we are to approach life God's way, listening to the guidance of the Spirit inside of us and obeying his voice speaking through the Word of God as we read and study it. We can depend on the greater power within us to be our master for obedience to God.

Made alive...no longer dead

The restoration of life is God's solution to every person's state of spiritual death. The Spirit of God enters the human spirit and brings eternal life with him.

Because of God's great love for us, he takes people like you and I who were once spiritually dead and makes us alive in Christ. It is his love that does this. It is his grace that gives this. It is his power that makes this happen. What a gift!

Dwell on the FACT that God's life is now indwelling you forever. You are alive in Christ. Christ is alive in you. Now you can enjoy the life given to you by Christ himself as your power for daily Christian living. In this life, you will experience freedom and joy. Dance! Shout! Sing!

20. *Graceful Living:* Give an illustration as to how living in a humble, teachable manner, saying no to sin, might look in someone's daily life (perhaps yours). Consider an everyday situation in which the old slave master "sin" tempts you.

21. *Graceful Living:* As a believer, you should know with confidence that God's life is now indwelling you forever. As you consider the condition of the "natural man" you learned earlier in the lesson, thank God for his indescribable gift of life to you. What are the benefits of having his life in you?

Respond to God about what he has shown you today.

DAY FOUR STUDY

As Ian Thomas said, "Jesus Christ **laid down** his life **for** you so that he could **give** his life **to** you so that he could **live** his life **through** you." All this is possible because of Christ's finished work on the cross and his resurrection on the third day. (See the chart below for a review.) We will continue our study of how he "lives his life through you" in the next lesson.

The Completed Work of the Cross and Resurrection

Jesus' Work	Need Addressed	Result
Propitiation	The just wrath of God against our sin.	God's just wrath is fully **satisfied**. He is **no longer angry** at your sin.
Reconciliation	Our state of alienation from God because of sin.	Your relationship with God is **restored...no longer broken**.
Redemption	Our state of slavery to sin and death.	You have been purchased and **released...no longer in bondage** to sin.
Forgiveness	Our guilt of sin before a holy God	You are **forgiven...no longer burdened by your sin**. Your guilt has been taken away.
Justification	Our need for perfect acceptability before a holy God.	You are **righteous...no longer guilty.** You are declared righteous in God's eyes.
Sanctification	Our need to be separated *from* the world, and *to* God—to be holy.	You are **perfected...no longer flawed** in God's sight. You are made holy for God's purposes.
Regeneration	Our state of spiritual death.	You have been **made alive** spiritually through the indwelling Holy Spirit. You are **no longer dead**.

22. *Graceful Living:* As you did before, write how you would explain **regeneration** (what the concept means for the believer, not necessarily the definition of the word) to someone who has not done this study but needs to know what they have in Christ.

REGENERATION—How would you explain "regeneration" to a new Christian? Even in difficult circumstances, why should "regeneration" make a difference in her life?

Respond to God about what he has shown you today.

Recommended: Listen to the podcast "Made Alive…No Longer Dead" after doing this lesson to reinforce what you have learned. Use the following listener guide.

Made Alive…No Longer Dead

JESUS' RESURRECTION IS THE GREATEST SUPERNATURAL EVENT IN HUMAN HISTORY!

- The empty tomb and the appearances of Jesus together are powerful evidence of the fact of Jesus' resurrection. When the early Christians spoke of Jesus being raised from the dead, they were claiming that something happened to Jesus, which had happened to no one else ever! God raised His Son from the dead and gave Him a new physical body that would never die again.

- Do you know why Jesus had to rise from the dead? Why is the physical bodily resurrection of Jesus Christ essential to our faith?

WHAT THE RESURRECTION DID NOT MEAN

- The resurrection was **not** meant to prove life after death.

- The resurrection was **not** the appearance of Jesus' spirit or ghost. The term "resurrection" in that day and time meant receiving a new physical body after a time of death. It was never a way of talking about a ghost or spirit.

- The resurrection also does **not** directly prove that Jesus is God. But the resurrection declared that what He did in His life and in His death was the work of God's Son.

- Jesus had to rise from the dead because His resurrection had several purposes in the plan of God.

PURPOSE #1 FOR JESUS' RESURRECTION—TO ANNOUNCE THE BEGINNING OF THE KINGDOM

- The Jews expected the resurrection to happen before the kingdom was established. They just didn't know that it would be a two-stage process—first, the Messiah resurrected, then later everyone else. *Daniel 12:2-3; Isaiah 26:19; John 5:28-29*

PURPOSE #2 FOR JESUS' RESURRECTION—TO GIVE ALL BELIEVERS HOPE FOR OUR FUTURE.

We get hope from knowing about Jesus' resurrected body.

- What stayed the same? Jesus looked like a normal human (not glowing). He talked, walked and preached a sermon at the same time, and had memory. He referred to Himself as having flesh and blood, could be touched, and could use His hands to eat.

- What was different? Sometimes it was hard to recognize Him. Jesus could appear and disappear at will. His body was physically robust after being severely beaten and crucified.

- Jesus is reigning over His Kingdom from heaven as God-man UNTIL He returns to set up His kingdom on earth. *Acts 1:9-11*

Jesus' resurrection gives us hope for our future.

- The Bible teaches that when you as a believer die, you go immediately to be with Jesus. *Luke 23:43; Philippians 1:23; 2 Corinthians 5:8-9; John 17:24*

- You will be in God's hand, in a prepared place, where you will receive comfort and be recognizable. *Acts 7:59-60; John 14:2-3; Luke 16:19-31; Revelation 6:9-11*

- You will get a resurrected human body like His. Perfect, sinless, robust, and designed for eternal life.

PURPOSE #3 FOR JESUS' RESURRECTION—PROVIDING A SOLUTION TO OUR STATE OF SPIRITUAL DEATH.

The need for life

- All humans are born spiritually dead in need of life. *Ephesians 2:1-3, 12*

- Jesus said that He came to give us life, abundant and full. We are made alive in Christ and are a new creation from that moment onward. *John 3:3-6; 5:24; 10:10; Ephesians 2:5; 2 Corinthians 5:17*

Restoration of life by the indwelling Holy Spirit

- It is the Holy Spirit who makes our spirits alive through His presence. *John 14:16-17*

- Resurrection brings life. And this life of Christ is in you. "Christ in you" is a fact of your new existence. *Colossians 1:27*

- We are **made alive…no longer dead**. This begins a new adventure of learning how to live with Christ in us and depending upon Him to do anything of value.

You are made alive…no longer dead.

- Because of God's great love for us, you can know and live with confidence that God's life is now indwelling you forever. You are alive in Christ. Christ is alive in you. Now you can enjoy the life given to you by Christ Himself.

- The resurrection of Jesus Christ is the greatest event in human history. Life-changing. Life-giving. Because of His resurrection, we get eternal spiritual life now and the promise of eternal physical life in our future—a new physical body that far exceeds anything we have ever known here. And this same Jesus is in His physical human body in heaven waiting for us to join Him there some day. That is hope!

Let Jesus satisfy your heart with His grace so that your life overflows with His grace every day. You will experience a life of freedom and joy!

6: Grace-Created Identity

"Therefore, if anyone is in Christ, he is a new creation; the old has gone, the new has come!" (2 CORINTHIANS 5:17)

Ask the Lord Jesus to speak to you through His Word each day. Tell Him you are listening.

DAY ONE STUDY

A new identity that rocks the world

In our world, identity drives everything about life. You likely carry some kind of identity card (ID) with you—a driver's license or a work-related card. What is on it? Usually, it is your name and picture, some identifying characteristics like address or job title, and the authority that issued the ID to you. Often, your signature is on the card representing your choice to enter into contract with the issuing authority. If someone asked, "Who are you?" you could answer with the information on that card.

Identities tell us who we are, where we live, how and where we can travel. Our identity drives what we can buy with our finances and qualifies us for employment. That is why we are so devastated when it is stolen! Knowing our spiritual identity is even more important.

> **Focus on the Meaning:** The government offers a "Witness Protection" program to those who testify against organized crime. The witnesses, helpless against the revenge of the criminals, receive a new identity and all the details that go along with it—new name, new background, new address, and new career. They can never go back to being what they were before. That is what God does for us. We each have a new spiritual identity. And there are wonderful perks to discover about our new position in life.

Yes, when you trusted in Christ, you received a new spiritual identity. But don't expect the culture to validate your new identity. From a worldly point of view, you and I are the same as we have always been. All our "baggage" is still seen hanging around our necks. But the FACT is that every Christian is a new creation with a new identity in Christ. This new identity declares how God, who is our authority, now views us! It is what he has done for us and to us that really counts, not what the culture thinks of us or what we think of ourselves. And there are wonderful perks that go along with this new position in life.

So far, you have learned how your faith in Jesus Christ sets you free from your previous sin-stained existence to enjoy a new life. But your ability to live out this freedom depends upon your understanding of who you now are.

How we see ourselves directs how we live our faith walk. We need to grasp the FACT that every believer gets a **new life** with a **radical** new identity—something we never had before, and something no one before Jesus' resurrection ever had!! And this new identity sets us free to live a radically new kind of life—a joyful life.

But not knowing our identity enslaves us to shoddy thinking and behavior. Many Christians through the years only knew they could have their sins forgiven and go to heaven when they died. And even then, they were not sure of that. The information about who they were in God's sight got lost in 2 things: (1) illiteracy of the Bible—lack of education and knowledge of what it actually says, and (2) slavery to poor teaching that one has to live by the church's rules to maintain God's acceptance—any church.

About 500 years ago, Martin Luther and other faithful believers who followed him rediscovered this identity treasure by reading and studying the Scriptures. For 300 years after that, believers were taught their identity in Christ before the teaching waned. Once again, a Christian was mainly someone who had her sins forgiven and went to heaven when she died, as long as she lived by certain rules to maintain God's acceptance. Many were enslaved once again to illiteracy of the Bible and poor teaching.

Because a great "Grace Awakening" has taken place since the 1970s, teaching about our new identity in Christ is everywhere in bookstores and on the radio, TV, and Internet. Yet, most believers still have no idea what their new identity is and all the benefits that come with it. Do you? And if you and I don't know who we are, how will we know we have been set free to live a different kind of life?

This lesson will certainly fill your mind and heart with truth about your grace-created new identity— an identity that will fill your life with freedom and joy!

The basis of identity

1. Think of some ways you try (or have tried in the past) to establish your identity apart from Christ. What happens when you try to determine who you are by these things?

2. From God's point of view, there are two kinds of people in the world: (1) those who are **in Adam**, and (2) those who are **in Christ**. Read the following verses. Using colored pens or pencils, mark anything related to being in Adam with one color. Mark anything related to being in Christ with a different color. Include the consequences of being *in Adam* and being *in Christ*.

   For since death came through a man, the resurrection of the dead comes also through a man. For as in Adam all die, so in Christ all will be made alive. (1 Corinthians 15:21-22)

   Therefore, just as sin entered the world through one man, and death through sin, and in this way death came to all people, because all sinned—To be sure, sin was in the world before the law was given, but sin is not charged against anyone's account where there is no law. Nevertheless, death reigned from the time of Adam to the time of Moses, even over those who did not sin by breaking a command, as did Adam, who is a pattern of the one to come. (Romans 5:12-14)

   But the gift is not like the trespass. For if the many died by the trespass of the one man, how much more did God's grace and the gift that came by the grace of the one man, Jesus Christ, overflow to the many! Nor can the gift of God be compared with the result of one man's sin: The judgment followed one sin and brought condemnation, but the gift followed many trespasses and brought justification. For if, by the trespass of the one man, death reigned through that one man, how much more will those who receive God's abundant provision of grace and of the gift of righteousness reign in life through the one man, Jesus Christ! (Romans 5:15-17)

   Consequently, just as one trespass resulted in condemnation for all people, so also one righteous act resulted in justification and life for all people. For just as through the disobedience of the one man the many were made sinners, so also through the obedience of the one man the many will be made righteous. (Romans 5:18-19)

The law was brought in so that the trespass might increase. But where sin increased, grace increased all the more, so that, just as sin reigned in death, so also grace might reign through righteousness to bring eternal life through Jesus Christ our Lord. (Romans 5:20-21)

- According to 1 Corinthians 15:21-22, what are the differences between being in Adam and being in Christ?

- Based on Romans 5:12-19, what are the results associated with being in Adam?

- From Romans 5:15-21, what are the results of being in Christ?

Who you are **in** determines your identity and your inheritance.

(1) To be **in Adam** means that you have inherited his nature (sinful), the consequences of his actions (condemnation), and his destiny (death).

(2) To be **in Christ** means that you have inherited his nature (righteous), the consequences of his actions (justification), and his destiny (eternal life).

3. *Graceful Living:* How you see yourself will influence how you think and live. How do you see yourself? In Christ? Or as just another one of the billions of human beings walking around on our planet? Reflect on how the way you see yourself (past and present) influences your life.

God has changed your identity through the baptism of the Holy Spirit

The word translated *baptized* came from the process for dyeing cloth. It did not matter if the cloth was sprayed, dipped, or immersed. The significance was taking on the identity of the dye. So in Spirit Baptism, we are "dyed" with Christ. The practical outcome is a total identification (uniting) with him.

4. Read Romans 6:1-11. List all the ways we are identified (united) with Christ in this passage. [Note: Although water baptism is a picture of what the Spirit does to us, there is no mention of water in this passage. Spirit baptism is much more significant and has far greater effects.]

   • Vv. 1-4—

   • Vv. 5-7—

   • Vv. 8-11—

5. According to Ephesians 2:4-6, in what are we united (identified) with Christ?

Through the baptism of the Holy Spirit—of which water baptism is a picture—the Christian has been totally identified with Jesus Christ. We are united with him in his death, in his resurrection, and in his ascension.

The Greek word translated "united" in Romans 6:5 literally means, "to make to grow together, to fuse." Being united with Christ, therefore, means that we become *fused together with him*. Consider items that are fused together such as fabrics or welded metal. The purpose of the fusing is usually to create something stronger, thicker, and holding together better than the original items.

At our moment of fusing, we are no longer on our own, but Jesus' transforming life-giving power now lives in us. We are now connected to the King who has supreme power and authority. Our lives are stronger and fulfill a greater purpose than what we could have done before the fusing.

John Wesley, the great 18th century Methodist preacher, said this, "Never think of yourself apart from Christ." We are continually **fused together** with him and can live to enjoy the benefits of being in him. Being united with Christ is part of your new identity.

6. ***Graceful Living:*** Reread Ephesians 2:4-6 below, inserting your name in the blanks.

But because of his great love for _____, God, who is rich in mercy,

made _____ alive with Christ even when you were dead in

transgressions—it is by grace you have been saved. And God raised

_____ up with Christ and seated _____

with him in the heavenly realms in Christ Jesus…

Dwell on what it means to you to be made alive and united with Christ.

Respond to God about what he has shown you today.

DAY TWO STUDY

Benefits of being identified with Christ

The moment we believe, the old self that was born **in Adam** died; a new self with the same body but a new interior started life as a new person with a new nature and a new inheritance. This radical new identity means you can never go back to not being **in Christ**. Ever!

Your new identity in Christ contains ~36 characteristics or benefits. You receive **all of these benefits at once** at the moment of your salvation because you are **in Christ**. God is not a vending machine, parceling out these benefits one at a time. They are God's gift based on his love for you. What God does to you is his choice, not yours. These benefits are **unconditional**. The burden of performance is upon God, not upon you.

We have already covered 7 aspects of your new identity in Christ. These are true about you because of Christ's finished work on the cross and his resurrection.

- Propitiation, safe from the wrath of God, freed from his anger (Romans 5:9,1 John 2:2)

- Reconciled to God (Romans 5:10)

- Redeemed (Ephesians 1:7)

- Forgiven, washed clean (Colossians 2:13-14; 1 Corinthians 6:11)

- Justified, declared righteous, given Christ's righteousness, and freed from condemnation / judgment (Romans 3:23-24; 2 Corinthians 5:21; Romans 8:1))

- Sanctified, made holy and blameless, perfect forever (1 Corinthians 6:11; Colossians 1:22; Hebrews 10:14)

- Translated out of death into life, indwelt by the Holy Spirit, born again, and made into a new creation (John 5:24; Romans 8:9; 1 Peter 1:3; 2 Corinthians 5:17)

Over the next two days, we will cover the other parts of your new identity.

7. Read the truth describing what is true about who you are. Look up the verses and reflect on what that means to you now. You are…

- Chosen by God (Ephesians 1:4)—

- Saved by Grace (Ephesians 2:8-9)—

- Made at peace with God (Romans 5:1)—

- Freed from the Law (Romans 7:4)—

- Accepted by God (Romans 15:7)—

- Made children of God, adopted as sons and heirs (John 1:12; Romans 8:14-17)—

- Given confident access to God (Hebrews 10:19-23)—

- Secure in God's Love (Romans 8:38-39)—

8. *Graceful Living:* One of the fundamental questions of the human race is that of identity, "Who am I?" The one secure, eternal answer is that through faith in Jesus Christ you can say, "I am in Christ, a child of God, one of God's saints, totally loved and accepted by God"— an identity that no circumstance can change! Write a short description of your identity in Christ based on what you discovered in the verses you just read. "I _____ *(your name)* am in Christ…"

Respond to God about what he has shown you today.

DAY THREE STUDY

Let us continue reading the truth about your identity in Christ.

9. Read the truth describing what is true about who you are. Look up the verses and reflect on what that means to you now. You are…

- Transferred out of darkness into light (Ephesians 5:8)—

- Made into a temple of the Holy Spirit (1 Corinthians 6:19)—

- Baptized into Christ's body, the Church (1 Corinthians 12:13)—

- Clothed with Christ (Galatians 3:27)—

- Sealed in Christ (Ephesians 1:13-14)—

- Made complete (Colossians 2:9-10)—

- Given every spiritual blessing (2 Peter 1:3)—

- Made citizens of heaven (Philippians 3:20-21)—

- Made into a holy and royal priesthood (1 Peter 2:5,9)—

A list containing the 36 characteristics of your new identity is found in the RESOURCES at the end of this book. Keep that handy for a quick reference when you are attacked by the world's view of who you are!

10. **Graceful Living:** Write a short description of your identity in Christ based on what you discovered in the verses you just read. "I _____ (your name) am in Christ,

Respond to God about what he has shown you today.

DAY FOUR STUDY

Knowing your identity sets you free from the world's viewpoint

As stated before, the world is not going to validate your new identity. From a worldly point of view, you are viewed as the same you have always been—with the baggage still hanging around your neck. But you can know your true identity—what God has done to change you from the inside out. And knowing it sets you free from the world's constraints and expectations, from your past, and from the garbage that others feed you about your failures.

> **Think About It:** "Some of us are drawn in by circumstance [wearing ourselves out by our own efforts] because we don't know who we are. The greatest crisis is not outside; it's the identity crisis within those of the faith! Men and women of God are so focused on the darkness that they're missing the adventure." (Michelle Wallace, "Fruit of the Vine: The Greatness of God," *Living Magazine,* October 2012)

11. ***Graceful Living:*** Read the chart below contrasting the world's **lies** about who you are with the FACT of God's **truth** about who you are. (Adapted from Dr. Timothy Warner, *Resolving Spiritual Conflicts and Cross-Cultural Ministry,* Freedom in Christ Ministries, 1993.)

The World's Lies (are)	God's Truth (says)
• You are still a sinner because you sometimes sin.	• You are a saint (one declared righteous by God) who sometimes sins.
• You get your identity from what you have done.	• You get your identity from what God has done for you.
• You get your identity from what people say about you.	• You get your identity from what God says about you.
• Your behavior tells you what to believe about yourself.	• Your belief about yourself directs your behavior.

Respond through any means you choose (journaling, prayer, poem, art, song) to illustrate what you have learned from this lesson.

> **Recommended:** Listen to the podcast "Lavished with Treasure in Christ" after doing this lesson to reinforce what you have learned. Use the following listener guide.

Lavished with Treasure in Christ

"It is as though (Paul) was ecstatically opening a treasure chest, lifting its jewels with his hands, letting them cascade through his fingers, and marveling briefly at them as they caught his eye." (*Dr. Constable's Notes on Ephesians 2019 Edition,* p. 15 regarding Ephesians 1:3-14)

WE RECEIVE EVERY SPIRITUAL BLESSING IN THE HEAVENLY REALMS (EPHESIANS 1:3)

- These blessings are associated with the heavenly realms—the unseen world of spiritual reality. God and all angelic beings, both good and bad, operate in this unseen dimension. *John 3; 2 Kings 2:11; 6:8-17; Daniel 9:21-23; 10:12-14; Matthew 26:53*

- When Christ was raised from the dead and ascended into heaven, He was exalted over all the powers there in the unseen world—angels, demons, and Satan. We as believers, all of us (the Church), join Christ there. *Ephesians 1:20-22; 2:6; 3:10*

BLESSING JEWEL IN EPHESIANS 1:4—CHOSEN TO BE HOLY AND BLAMELESS

- **To be chosen** does mean that God had a plan from the beginning for all believers to be in Christ and to be made holy and blameless in Him. We are not told how God knows beforehand who will believe in Him. And God commands all people to believe and that the gospel is to be preached to all people. Whether Jew or Gentile, all Christians are now called chosen. *Acts 16:31; 1 Timothy 2:4; Matthew 28:18-20; Deuteronomy 29:29*

- **To be chosen** does not mean that God chose some people to love and some to not love before any were ever born. God loves everyone, and everyone can believe in Him. *John 3:16; Romans 8:38-39*

BLESSING JEWEL IN EPHESIANS 1:5—PREDESTINED TO BE ADOPTED AS SONS & HEIRS

- **Predestined** does mean that God determined beforehand that all believers would be adopted as His sons & daughters with full inheritance rights.

- **Predestined** does not mean that you are a puppet with no control over your "destiny." Individuals choose to be for Him and receive all spiritual blessings plus heaven or choose against Him and receive nothing plus eternal separation from God.

BLESSING JEWELS IN EPHESIANS 1:6-8—REDEMPTION, FORGIVENESS, & LAVISHED WITH GRACE

- To lavish means "to bestow something in generous or extravagant quantities." God's grace is poured out upon us richly. He lavishes us with it though we don't deserve such favor. Grace is summed up in the name, person, and work of the Lord Jesus Christ. We receive this favor or acceptance from God as a free gift through faith in Christ.

BLESSING JEWEL IN EPHESIANS 1:9-10—REVELATION

- God has made known to us a mystery that was kept in the heart of God until Christ came. Part of the mystery being revealed is that the Gentiles and Jews are joined together through the gospel into one body, the Body of Christ. *Ephesians 3:6*

- Another part of God's plan for the future has been revealed to us so we can know it. His future plan will bring all things in heaven and on earth together under the headship of Christ. We know the what, but we do not know the when.

- God give us this revelation to give us hope as we live in this fallen world.

THE BLESSING JEWEL OF BEING SEALED AND SECURED BY THE HOLY SPIRIT (EPHESIANS 1:13-14)

- A seal was a common thing in Paul's day that carried with it the idea of ownership, identification, security, permanence, and completeness.

- God marks His people as His own through the presence of the Holy Spirit in their lives.
  - ✓ His seal means we are wanted, valuable and important.
  - ✓ Being sealed gives us continued assurance that we are God's children and will receive all the inheritance promised to His children—such as heaven, new bodies, and living with Christ in His kingdom. There is no power greater than God who could break the seal, including yourself.
  - ✓ Sealing also communicates that the contents are prepared and complete. All those gifts of the cross prepare and complete us.
  - ✓ Sealing takes place the moment you believe in Christ for salvation for all believers. No exception is given. It is immediate and permanent.
  - ✓ God the Father does the sealing; the Holy Spirit is the seal. Nowhere are we exhorted to ask for it so it must be universal and immediate.

- We are guaranteed all that God has promised for our future. The Holy Spirit being present within us assures us that we are God's, that He won't forget about us when Jesus returns, that we go to be with Him when we die, that our sins will never again count against us, that we are new creatures and that all those truths about our identity in Christ are ours forever.

- Let your heart overflow in praise and thanksgiving for those blessing jewels which are in your Treasure in Christ. Use prayer, prose, poetry, drawing, song or whatever you choose.

Let Jesus satisfy your heart with His grace so that your life overflows with His grace every day. You will experience a life of freedom and joy!

7: Grace-Based Freedom

"The only thing I want to learn from you is this: Did you receive the Spirit by doing the works of the law or by believing what you heard? Are you so foolish? Although you began with the Spirit, are you now trying to finish by human effort? Have you suffered so many things for nothing? – if indeed it was for nothing. Does God then give you the Spirit and work miracles among you by your doing the works of the law or by your believing what you heard?" (GALATIANS 3:2-5)

Ask the Lord Jesus to speak to you through His Word each day. Tell Him you are listening.

DAY ONE STUDY

Introduction to Law and Grace

[Note: This lesson contains more teaching than usual to clearly communicate this topic.]

You have a great foundation now, knowing what Christ has done on the cross for you and how his resurrection made the way for you to receive the gift of life with a new identity. Praise God for his indescribable gift!

Many Christians start out accepting the gift of salvation by grace. But through poor teaching, they are thrown into a *works-related* way of living out this new life in order to maintain acceptance before a holy God. This may have been your experience. The issue is broadly called "Law and Grace."

Understanding the difference between "law" and "grace" answers frequently asked questions such as these: What is the difference between the Old and New Testaments? How are we to live to please God after we are saved? What works must we do to stay saved?

Most importantly, understanding the difference between "law" and "grace" is the foundation of the gospel you received and the basis for you to experience a life full of freedom and joy. Christ's finished work on the cross and his resurrection show you how to approach life God's way in three particular areas of living out your Christian life: motivation, power, and relationships.

Consider these questions for yourself to see how much you have been influenced by a works-related way of living out your Christian life.

- Is your **motivation** to live the Christian life and please God based on fear of what God will do to you every time you fail? Or is it based on love and gratitude for what Christ has done for you?

- Do you think the **power** to live the Christian life is through self-effort (try hard enough)? Or is it Spirit-empowered (trusting in the Spirit to enable you to do so)?

- In your **relationships** with others, do you try to motivate others to obedience through fear of punishment—given out by God or by you? Or do you recognize the grace God has shown you so you encourage others to obedience out of hearts of love and gratitude?

So understanding the difference between "law" and "grace" will help you to recognize the wrong approach to life and direct you to God's way of approaching life. The result is a life of freedom and joy.

Probably the simplest way to understand Law & Grace is to see it as the issue of God's acceptance: "On what basis are you made acceptable before a holy God?" Based upon what you have learned so far in this study, how would you answer that question?

Because this tension between law and grace has been going on since the early days of the Church, let us first get a good handle on what is meant by "the Law" in the Bible.

What is "The Law?"

Reading through the New Testament, you will often see this phrase, "the Law." Generally, the New Testament writers mean "the Mosaic Law" by this phrase. The Law is, "The covenant between God and the nation of Israel instituted at Mt. Sinai after the Exodus from Egypt." Though not capitalized in most translations, "the law" is referring to the Law of Moses.

Here's a brief recap of what that means.

> **Scriptural Insight:** In Genesis 12:1-3, God promised to Abraham (400 years before Moses) that he would make Abraham into a great nation and that all the peoples on earth would be blessed through Abraham. Abraham's descendants multiplied greatly while living in Egypt, and God delivered them out of Egypt to form the nation he had promised to Abraham. At Mt. Sinai, God proposed a contractual agreement (the Law) to the new nation (Exodus 19:3-6). After God spoke the outline of the Law (the Ten Commandments) and the provisions of the Law to the people (Exodus 20-23), the nation agreed to keep the contract (Exodus 24:3-8).
>
> From the simplest, big-picture point of view, the Law of Moses [Mosaic Law, hereafter designated as the Law] described the conditions under which: 1) Israel would be allowed to dwell in the land, and 2) the people of Israel would enjoy the presence of God dwelling in their midst. The Law was bilateral (two-sided), meaning that God offered earthly blessings for obedience and earthly curses for disobedience (Deuteronomy 28). The Law was not a means of salvation. The Law was primarily *national* in scope and *earthly* in application.

Why did God give the Law?

Now, let us see what the New Testament says about the Law.

1. Read the following verses. Mark whatever is revealed about the purpose and duration of the Law. Then, answer the questions below.

    [19] Why, then, was the law given at all? It was added because of transgressions until the Seed to whom the promise referred had come. The law was given through angels and entrusted to a mediator. [20] A mediator, however, implies more than one party; but God is one. [21] Is the law, therefore, opposed to the promises of God? Absolutely not! For if a law had been given that could impart life, then righteousness would certainly have come by the law. [22] But Scripture has locked up everything under the control of sin, so that what was promised, being given through faith in Jesus Christ, might be given to those who believe. [23] Before the coming of this faith, we were held in custody under the law, locked up until the faith that was to come would be revealed. [24] So the law was our guardian until Christ came that we might be justified by faith. [25] Now that this faith has come, we are no longer under a guardian. [26] So in Christ Jesus you are all children of God through faith, (Galatians 3:19-26)

    *   Why did God give the Law (v. 19)?

    *   What did not come by the Law (v. 21)?

- What was the intended duration for the Law (v. 24)?

- What did the Law do until that time?

Four hundred years before the Law was given to Israel, God promised to Abraham (Genesis 12:1-3) that he would redeem human beings from their sin based on his grace. That promise of grace was not nullified or changed by the giving of the Law. The Law—a separate arrangement for a temporary purpose—was for managing sinful people until fulfillment in Christ (see diagram below).

God's Promise of Redemption
through the Redeemer

The giving of the Law to Israel had several purposes:

- To make the nation of Israel into a holy nation as God was a holy God. *"Be holy because I, the Lord your God, am holy" (Leviticus 19:2).* For a person to be holy required separation from sin. Therefore, much of the Law includes animal sacrifices for the sin of the people so God could remove their sins from them (Leviticus 16:20-22), making them holy again.

- To teach central truths about God. There had to be a nation on earth that knew something about God to teach the rest of the world (Deuteronomy 4:5-8).

- To protect and preserve Israel as a distinct people through whom the promised Messiah would come to bless the whole world.

- To lead people to a trust relationship with the Lord, thus preparing the way for the work of Christ. The Law showed people their sin, leaving faith in the mercy and grace of God alone to forgive one's guilt and be right with God (Romans 3:19-20). Salvation for Old Testament believers came through **faith in a merciful God** (Habakkuk 3:17) not through the Law.

Why was there a need for a New Covenant?

Because the Law had limitations, God promised a New Covenant. The Jews knew about the New Covenant God promised in Jeremiah 31:31-34. When Jesus spoke about the New Covenant the night before he died, this is what he was referencing.

2. Read Hebrews 8:7-13, which quotes the promise in Jeremiah.

    *   Why did God make a New Covenant (vv. 7-9)?

    *   Why would the New Covenant be better (vv. 10-12)?

    *   What would happen to the Old Covenant (v. 13)?

The New Covenant proclaims freedom from those Old Testament laws (sacrifices, circumcision, diet) for both Gentiles and Jews based upon what Christ did on the cross to fulfill the purpose for the Old Testament religious laws. You learned all about that in Lessons 3 and 4.

Because believers have a change of heart and the Holy Spirit's presence inside, the motivation to please God is internal rather than external as with the Law. This promotes transparency in our relationship with God and helps us to obey our God better. Our acceptance before God is not based on our never messing up. It is God's choice to hold onto us because we are in Christ. Under this New Covenant, we get to know God personally regardless of our status in life because our relationship with God is based upon our faith in Jesus Christ. And our sins are not just covered but are taken away forever.

Under the Law (Old Covenant), blessings were *conditional* and the burden of performance was on *humans.* Under the New Covenant, the promised blessings are *unconditional* and the burden of performance is upon *God.* The sole responsibility of humans toward the fulfillment of the New Covenant is to enter into that relationship through faith in Jesus Christ. God then **commits himself** to complete the work he began in us (Philippians 1:6) until we are conformed to the image of his Son (Romans 8:29). This does not mean that Christians have no responsibilities at all! We are called to follow Jesus Christ diligently and live worthy of our calling (Ephesians 4:1).

I know we have covered a lot in this section. But all that you have learned lays a foundation for the rest of the lesson. So stay with it. ☺

3. ***Graceful Living:*** What did you learn about the Old and New Covenants today that you did not already know?

Respond to God about what he has shown you today.

DAY TWO STUDY

God's plan for something new

Before Christ, Gentiles who put their faith in God would join the Jewish faith and start obeying the Mosaic Law. Then they could be acceptable to God. Some Jewish Christians, especially those who had been leaders in Jewish teaching, thought it still worked that way in the Church. But God had a new plan and a different goal.

4. Read the verses below. Mark everything related to God's new plan. Then answer the questions that follow.

> *[11] Therefore, remember that formerly you who are Gentiles by birth and called "uncircumcised" by those who call themselves "the circumcision" (which is done in the body by human hands)— [12] remember that at that time you were separate from Christ, excluded from citizenship in Israel and foreigners to the covenants of the promise, without hope and without God in the world. [13] But now in Christ Jesus you who once were far away have been brought near by the blood of Christ. [14] For he himself is our peace, who has made the two groups one and has destroyed the barrier, the dividing wall of hostility, [15] by setting aside in his flesh the Law with its commands and regulations. his purpose was to create in himself one new humanity out of the two, thus making peace, [16] and in one body to reconcile both of them to God through the cross, by which he put to death their hostility. [17] he came and preached peace to you who were far away and peace to those who were near. [18] For through him we both have access to the Father by one Spirit. [19] Consequently, you are no longer foreigners and strangers, but fellow citizens with God's people and also members of his household, [20] built on the foundation of the apostles and prophets, with Christ Jesus himself as the chief cornerstone. [21] In him the whole building is joined together and rises to become a holy temple in the Lord. [22] And in him you too are being built together to become a dwelling in which God lives by his Spirit. (Ephesians 2:11-22)*

> *In reading this, then, you will be able to understand my insight into the mystery of Christ, which was not made known to people in other generations as it has now been revealed by the Spirit to God's holy apostles and prophets. This mystery is that through the gospel the Gentiles are heirs together with Israel, members together of one body, and sharers together in the promise in Christ Jesus. (Ephesians 3:4-6)*

*   What was the condition of the Gentiles before hearing of Christ (Ephesians 2:11-12)?

*   In Ephesians 2:14, Christ made the two groups (Jews and Gentiles) into one by breaking down the barrier of the dividing wall. What was the dividing wall (the first part of verse 15)?

*   What was Christ's purpose according to Ephesians 2:15-16?

- What are the results of this barrier coming down according to Ephesians 2:18-20?

- What was the mystery of Christ unknown to the Jews in the past but now being revealed (Ephesians 3:4-6)?

God's goal in the New Covenant is to make both groups into one (Ephesians 2:14, diagram at right). The Gentiles and the Jews would join the Church ("one new humanity out of the two") as equals and co-heirs of everything promised by God to all those who believe in Jesus Christ.

Christ broke down the dividing wall, the Law with its commandments and regulations, that separated the Jews from the Gentiles. The barrier had to come down so that Christ could create in himself a new humanity out of the two groups. He would reconcile both groups to God through the cross, not through the Law. As a result, there is peace between Jew and Gentile in Christ. Both have access to the Father by one Spirit. Both share together all the promises in Jesus Christ.

It is important to remember that the Mosaic Law was a covenant between God and the nation Israel only. At no time was it imposed on other nations of the world. The Old Testament frequently describes prophetically the blessings the whole world will receive through the Messiah (Christ) and his kingdom. But there was a great secret (a "mystery") held in the heart of God—that the Gentiles, who were held separate from the Jews by the Law, would be included in God's promises through the gospel of Jesus Christ. The mystery is now revealed. To God be the glory! Dance, shout, sing!

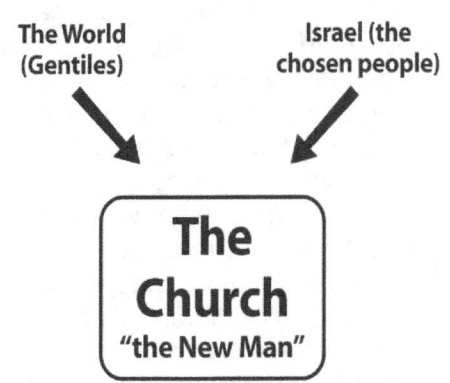

God's Goal:
"to make both groups into one" (Eph. 2:14)

The World (Gentiles)   **Israel (the chosen people)**

The Church
"the New Man"

to "reconcile them both in one body to God through the cross...for through Him we both have our access in one Spirit to the Father." (Eph. 2:16,18)

Old ways sneak into the new church

God's plan is too easy for many to accept. And old habits of works-based religion are hard to break. Soon, false teachers called "Judaizers" began telling the new Gentile Christians that they had to become Jews first, get circumcised and start obeying the Mosaic Law. Then, the Gentiles could be acceptable to God and receive salvation through faith in Christ. This stirred up a lot of controversy in the early church. Eventually, the controversy grew so heated that it was brought to Jerusalem to be decided by the apostles. Thankfully, God made sure it got cleared up and recorded the truth for us to know.

The Judaizers' message was basically this: "We have the promises, Christ, and salvation. If you want them, you must come over to our side." In their worldview, the Gentiles must become Jews first (Acts 15:1-5).

5. After open debate, the apostles under the inspiration of the Holy Spirit gave an answer to the Judaizers' position. Read Acts 15:6-11. What did the apostles conclude?

The apostolic council's decision confirmed God's new plan based on Peter's testimony of what he saw with his own eyes. The Gentiles and Jews are equally saved by faith in Christ alone and equally given the full blessings of salvation. The Law is no longer needed. It was a burdensome yoke upon the Jews for so many years. God's new plan was so much better!

Even though the apostles confirmed that the Gentile Christians did not have to become Jews and follow the Mosaic Law, the Judaizers did not give up. Their influence started reaching more and more of the new Gentile churches, including those begun by the missionary work of Paul and Barnabas in the area known as Galatia (central Turkey).

News reached Paul about this false teaching messing with the minds and hearts of the new believers in the Galatian churches. Paul addressed it with firmness and clarity. The book of Galatians as a whole was written to address the panic created by the Judaizers' teaching. Yet, the warnings and truths are applicable to anyone today who thinks you have to follow the Law to be true Christians.

Let us look at these truths.

6. Read Galatians 1:6-9. Who and what are the Galatians deserting?

7. Read Galatians 3:1-5. Paul asks the Galatians questions to draw out their poor thinking.

   • What did Paul ask the Galatians about how they received the Spirit in v. 2?

   • After beginning by means of the Spirit, what are they doing now (v. 3)?

   • What question did Paul ask them in v. 5?

8. Read Galatians 5:1-3. If Christ has set them free so they could enjoy that freedom, what should they not do and why?

Scriptural Insight: To "fall away" in v. 4 refers to getting away from living by grace and going back to living by law. This does not refer to loss of salvation.

Paul responded with conviction to anyone who thinks they must follow the Law to be true Christians. Following that kind of teaching is desertion of the gospel and no gospel at all. It is opposite what the gospel teaches. God works in us through his Spirit and by faith. Do not let anyone put you in that slavery again. Instead, live in your freedom through the Spirit. Live out your life based on grace.

How should Christians view the Law now?

9. According to Colossians 2:13-14, what happened to the Law (written code, "our legal indebtedness")?

Focus on the Meaning: The Law, the legal indebtedness that stood against us, was nailed to the cross. It was canceled. The word Paul used there meant destroyed, wiped away, erased, and blotted out. That sounds pretty permanent, doesn't it?

10. According to Romans 6:14 and 7:6, what is the Christian's relation to the Law now?

Believers are dead to the Law and are released from the Law. Released. The Law no longer comes into play regarding our living a life that pleases God. This is crucial to *graceful living!*

So if Christians are no longer under the Law of Moses in any way, shape or form, why read and study the Old Testament? Paul anticipates our question when he wrote this,

> *"All Scripture is God-breathed and is useful for teaching, rebuking, correcting and training in righteousness, so that the man of God may be thoroughly equipped for every good work." (2 Timothy 3:16-17)*

When Paul wrote those words under the guidance of the Holy Spirit, "all Scripture" at that time was the whole Old Testament. God has revealed himself through what is written—his holiness, goodness, sovereignty, omniscience, omnipotence, love and more. You see him working in and through real people. You see his love expressed for them.

For the people of Israel (and for Gentile converts who voluntarily took on the yoke of the Law), the Law served as their rule of life—**learning to approach life God's way**. The Law God gave to Israel included 3 aspects: civil (how to govern the nation), religious (how to worship a holy God), and moral (how to treat one another). Though Christians are not under the civil or religious laws given to Israel, God's moral law has not changed and is reinforced in New Testament writings.

So the Mosaic Law can be properly used as a **lens** through which to see the holiness of God. The Law can also be used as a **mirror** in which to see oneself truly in comparison to the holiness of God, especially the moral law (dealing with murder, marriage, relationships, etc.). It cannot clean you up, but it can reveal that you have a problem called sin (Romans 3:19-20; 1 Timothy 1:8-10).

But the Law cannot be used as a ladder on which to climb up to try to earn the acceptance of God or force others to do so. For example, Christians who choose to follow some of the commands God gave to Israel cannot guilt others into doing so in order to become "more godly," such as rules about food or the Sabbath.

By the time of Jesus, rabbis taught that the whole law could be summed up with two sentences,

> "...Love the Lord your God with all your heart and with all your soul and with all your strength and with all your mind'; and, 'Love your neighbor as yourself." (Luke 10:27)

That has not changed. The rest of the New Testament describes how to live that way.

11. **Graceful Living:** Based upon what you just learned, posting "The Ten Commandments" from Exodus 20 as your rule of life does give the wrong message to other believers or to the unbelieving world. Consider some New Testament verses that would be far more effective in communicating God's grace to an unbelieving world than posting the "Ten Commandments" (the Law).

12. **Deeper Discoveries (optional):** Which of the Ten Commandments (Exodus 20:2-17) ...

- Emphasize "Love the Lord your God" and are repeated in New Testament writings as the right way to live for one who is forgiven and redeemed? Give verses.

- Are related to God's moral law – how we are to treat one another – and repeated in New Testament writings as the right way to live as one who is forgiven and redeemed? Give verses.

- Is given specifically to Israel as a nation but not to the rest of the world, yet has been taught that it applies to the Church (and on the wrong day!)? See Colossians 2:16 regarding this one.

Respond to God about what he has shown you today.

DAY THREE STUDY

The tendency toward legalism in the modern church

You may be thinking, "What does this have to do with me?" Be aware that what happened to the Galatians is still present in the modern church. We call it "legalism" (legal = relating to the law). It is not likely that you will be pushed into following the Mosaic Law although some denominations do add parts of it to their own religious practices.

So what is legalism? Legalism **is the addition of any other conditions to faith in order to gain and maintain acceptance from God**, and even how to stay saved. Recognize it as "faith **plus**" other things, such as good works, refraining from certain sins, church membership, ordinances or sacraments (baptism, communion), etc. This is where you are likely to be wrongly influenced. *Whenever God's acceptance of you has an "IF" attached to it (other than faith in Jesus Christ), you know you are in the vicinity of legalism.*

This discussion of legalism is not about what is clearly taught as right and wrong from God's perspective in Scripture. That which God calls "sin" will be covered more in lesson 9.

13. ***Graceful Living:*** Do you recognize the influence of legalism in your own life? What "faith plus _____" teaching have you been taught to obey to remain acceptable to God?

14. Read the verses below. Mark anything that deals with human commands or adding rules to make one "more godly" and the effects of doing so. Then, answer the questions below.

Therefore do not let anyone judge you by what you eat or drink, or with regard to a religious festival, a New Moon celebration or a Sabbath day. These are a shadow of the things that were to come; the reality, however, is found in Christ. Do not let anyone who delights in false humility and the worship of angels disqualify you. Such a person also goes into great detail about what they have seen; they are puffed up with idle notions by their unspiritual mind. They have lost connection with the head, from whom the whole body, supported and held together by its ligaments and sinews, grows as God causes it to grow. Since you died with Christ to the elemental spiritual forces of this world, why, as though you still belonged to the world, do you submit to its rules: "Do not handle! Do not taste! Do not touch!"? These rules, which have to do with things that are all destined to perish with use, are based on merely human commands and teachings. Such regulations indeed have an appearance of wisdom, with their self-imposed worship, their false humility and their harsh treatment of the body, but they lack any value in restraining sensual indulgence. (Colossians 2:16-23)

- What warnings did Paul give?

- Rather than producing righteousness, what can legalism produce?

Paul warned the Colossians about legalistic practices and thinking that could affect their lives (what one eats or drinks, participation in religious festivals, and Sabbath requirements). He also mentioned anything that gives someone false humility such as "spiritual experiences" and focus on angels. Those experiences lead to pride (being puffed up) and a disconnect from the supremacy of Christ.

Continuing his discussion of living by the law (do not handle, taste or touch), Paul points out those activities lead to an appearance of wisdom but lack any value in controlling sinful sensual lusts.

Modern examples of legalism are rules that require you to listen to only certain kinds of music and not wear certain types of clothing. Legalism makes rules for when and how often you must attend church and what you are allowed to eat and drink to stay acceptable to God. Legalism declares certain activities sinful when God does not. Following such "checklists" can cause boasting and a hardened heart toward others who do not abide by such rules. They can even be illogical.

> **Think About It:** God gives a command with a certain intent. Humans add controls to the rule which leaves out God's intent.

The effects of living by law rather than by grace

Legalism leads to a dramatically different experience of Christian living. Many groups or individuals begin with a clear presentation of the gospel of grace to receive salvation, then proceed to live by works, trying to earn or maintain God's acceptance by performance. That would include insistence you follow the Mosaic Law, human "religious" laws imposed by others, or self-imposed rules that you feel make you more spiritual than others. The effects on the individual of any living by works are the same—fear, guilt, and condemnation.

A person is "living by law" (legalism) whenever she tries **to approach God on the basis of her own merits or performance.** Though the outward effects are often subtle, a believer trying to live by law will actually be drifting her focus away from the Person of Jesus Christ (Galatians 1:6; Colossians 2:19). She is straying from enjoying a relationship to practicing a religion. This is opposite of God's plan for you.

15. Why did God choose to give us salvation by his grace based on our faith alone (Ephesians 2:8-9)?

Out of God's mercy comes his **grace**. Remember that grace is unmerited favor. It is a gift that is undeserved. Grace is a gift God chooses to give because of his great love and mercy, apart from the Law (Romans 3:21). The Law (Mosaic or man-imposed religious standards) is incompatible with "Grace!" Like Jesus' example of pouring new wine into new wineskins rather than into old ones (Matthew 9:14-17), grace cannot be added to the Law. It is one or the other. You cannot accept both. Which one would you rather guide the course of your life? We will look at "living by grace" on Day Four.

> **Focus on the Meaning:** Transformation takes place in the context of grace. Grace is commonly defined as unmerited favor...an undeserved gift. We understand grace is required for salvation and yet too often, grace is forgotten afterwards. We move into a graceless-centered life and instead tie our spiritual growth to works-based performance. God cannot love us more, and he refuses to love us less. Performance does not earn salvation, love, transformation or spiritual growth. (Debby Rowe, *The Disciplemaking Ministry Guide,* "Navigate" page 9)

Why does legalism persist in the church?

The issue of "Law and Grace" often arises in practice because of two reasons: 1) the tendency to think you can control sin through lots of rules and 2) the persistent tendency to *interpret events.*

Regarding controlling sin through lots of rules, legalism is used to motivate people to obedience by fear of punishment. Paul showed in the Colossians passage you read above that adding rules may seem to control outward behavior but not sin in the heart. So how does that play into our tendency to interpret events.

Everyone must deal with disappointments, problems, and tragedies in life. The human tendency is to try to interpret events as signs of God's anger or favor, asking questions such as: *"Why did this happen? What does it mean? What is God trying to tell me?"*

Professing Christians may acknowledge grace as true but live as though their own performance of religious standards determines their fate in life. They live in fear of God, not a healthy fear, but an unhealthy one—a fear of what God will do to them every time they fail. That becomes the motivation for their Christian living—how to stay on the good side of God so bad things won't happen.

Why do some believers succumb to this thinking? The answer is that we do not understand the difference between *punishment* and *discipline.*

- Punishment is a penalty imposed on an offender for a crime or wrongdoing. Example: getting a speeding ticket, a jail sentence.

- Discipline is training that develops character, self-control, orderliness and/or efficiency. It is forward-looking to a change of behavior and/or character, is individually tailored, personally applied, and is chiefly concerned with what will benefit the individual in question. Discipline is **not** always corrective or applied in response to sin. It is ongoing. Think "training." Example: teaching children how to regularly brush their teeth.

Punishment and discipline sometimes look alike (especially to the one on the receiving end), but they are very different, especially for the Christian in her relation to God.

16. What do Romans 5:9 and 8:1 adamantly declare to you, as a believer, about freedom from the wrath (punishment) from God?

Review our discussion of "Propitiation" in Lesson 3, Day One Study. You are saved from the wrath of God (punishment for sin). He is completely satisfied by Christ's sacrifice on the cross. Because you trusted in Christ, God is no longer angry at you because of your sin. Delete that fear out of your mind whenever something not-so-good happens to you.

> **Think About It:** If you recognize that you have been relating to God out of a feeling of obligation, guilt, and fear of punishment for not doing it right, let that go. Accept his complete love and acceptance of you in Christ. Review what you learned in Lesson 3-6. Give that fear to God and trust him to replace it with confidence in his love for you.

As his child, God does discipline (train) you as he transforms you to become more like his Son (Romans 8:28-30).

17. Read the following verses. What or whom does God use to discipline his children?

- 2 Corinthians 1:8-9—

- 2 Timothy 2:24-26—

- 2 Timothy 3:16-17—

Because you live under the grace of God in Jesus Christ, you can rest in the fact that **all of God's purposes for you are good**. You have a loving Father who teaches, trains, and corrects. Even when evil occurs (because we still live in a fallen world), you can rest confidently in the promise of Romans 8:28: *"And we know that God causes all things to work together for good to those who love God, to those who are called according to his purpose."* Our God is good all the time to us— even in the tough times, in different ways to each of his children, and by what he allows and does not allow into our lives.

18. *Graceful Living:*

- Think back to your Christian life so far and try to recognize the influence of *legalism* on what you have been taught. If you have been taught any "faith plus any other condition" in order to maintain acceptance to God, get to heaven, or get any other blessing (which you already have in Christ!), consider how this has affected your life, emotions, thinking, or relationship with God and others. Then, let it go and cling to the truth of your identity in Christ.

- Consider the means that God has used to train (discipline) you to trust him more, to depend upon him more, and to say "no" to selfishness and "yes" to selflessness. In what ways are you grateful for those lessons that overflowed from his grace and love towards you even if they hurt?

Respond to God about what he has shown you today.

DAY FOUR STUDY

Living by grace motivates you to obedience out of love and gratitude

So why do some Christians so easily stray away from grace into legalism? Why would someone want to retain the Law or create additional laws for Christians to follow? Often, it is because of the fear of lawlessness. All agree that lawlessness is wrong and is to be opposed. Yet, there is the tendency to think sin can be controlled through lots of rules. We all know how much that does not work!

The answer, however, is not that we should keep believers under law. It is teaching and exhorting believers to "live by the Spirit"—the better way.

19. In contrast to living by law, how are Christians exhorted to live with our grace-based freedom (Galatians 5:13-16)?

20. According to Romans 5:8 and 2 Corinthians 5:14-15, what should motivate us to obey God with our lives if not legalism?

21. Read Romans 6:1-7. To those who take advantage of God's grace to indulge in sinful behavior knowing you will be forgiven, what is Paul's answer?

Through our adoption as sons and the gift of the Holy Spirit, we have received a status as spiritual *adults.* Adults live on the basis of *mature character* with FREEDOM and responsibility. Paul confirms that we are united with Christ with a new identity and status. Knowing your new status in Christ, based on all that Christ has done for you and what you have in him, helps to answer the question, "Why should I live a godly life if I'm not under law?"

The answer can simply be GRATITUDE for God's great LOVE for you. Romans 5:8 describes how much God loves you and how he demonstrated that love through Christ's death on the cross for you. Christ's love compels you to live for him because of what he did for you.

> **Scriptural Insight:** A preacher of the Law comes down on men with threats and punishments; a preacher of divine grace coaxes and urges men by reminding them of the goodness and mercy which God has shown them. For he [God] would have no unwilling workers nor cheerless service; he wants men to be glad and cheerful in the service of God. (Martin Luther, comments on Romans 12)

22. From Titus 2:11-14, what does grace teach us so we can reach God's goal of godliness in our lives?

Think About It: What God wants is for us to **trust** him and his Word—the Word that tells us that Christ has done it all—and to **act** on it by approaching 'the throne of grace with **confidence**, so that we may receive mercy and find grace to help in our time of need' (Hebrews 4:16) ...But if you don't trust that you have been made totally acceptable in God's sight, you will never have the boldness to approach him. You will linger outside his throne room, trying to find a way to get 'worthy' enough to go in. The end result is that you will avoid going to your only source of help (God) when you need him the most! (Bob George, *Classic Christianity*, page 102)

23. Read Philippians 3:3-10.

- How does Paul consider his early life living by Law compared to living by the grace of God (vv. 3-7)?

- What was of surpassing worth for him (verses 8-9)?

24. Read 1 Timothy 1:12-17. What did Paul learn about the value of grace in his life?

Paul understood the plight of those who had been relating to God through outward performance under the Law for years. He had been there! Those who have been freed from the Law (both Jews and non-Jews since Christ) can now have a relationship with God on the basis of his **grace**, as Paul describes about his own life (1 Timothy 1:12-17). **Grace motivates us to obedience by love and gratitude for what Christ has done.**

We have spent most of this lesson talking about our motivation for living the Christian life. In the next two lessons, we will talk about accessing the power available to us to live a life that pleases God. And we will discover how living by grace rather than by law influences our relationships with others.

25. **Graceful Living:** God wants you to relate to him on the basis of his grace, so that your motivation to obey him is based on his love for you, your love for him, and gratitude for what Christ has done for you. Relax! Thank him that you have FREEDOM to relate to your God on the basis of his Grace to you. And enjoy your Grace-filled relationship with your God today, tomorrow, and forever!

Paul responded to God's grace call on his life with a statement of praise in 1 Timothy 1:17. How will you respond? **Respond to God about what he has shown you today.** Feel free to use any creative means including drawing a diagram of your freedom in Christ now.

Recommended: Listen to the podcast "Balance Your Liberty with Love" after doing this lesson to reinforce what you have learned. Use the following listener guide.

Balance Your Liberty with Love

Christians are to be a love-bonded community. How well we love makes Jesus look good or bad. It is so important because that is what the outside world sees. And based on the impression we give them, they make a judgment about Jesus. It is our love-bond that brings glory to God.

BALANCING LIBERTY BEGINS WITH ACCEPTANCE (ROMANS 14:1; 15:7).

- Disputable matters are things not specifically stated as right or wrong, especially for Christians as stated in the New Testament. For any issue that arises, you can determine your response to that issue by asking 3 questions about that issue:

  ✓ Question 1: Is it a moral issue?
  ✓ Question 2: Is it stunting someone's spiritual growth?
  ✓ Question 3: Is it disrupting unity within the Body of Christ?

QUESTION 1: IS IT A MORAL ISSUE?

Absolutes are truths essential to the Christian faith. They never change.

- Absolutes are true for every believer, in every nation, in every culture, and during every time period in history.

- *Absolute doctrines* are those defining true Christianity, and they are non-negotiable. Examples are: The Bible is the inspired Word of God. God is a Trinity: Three Persons in One. Jesus is God, not just a human religious teacher. Jesus died and rose from the grave for the sins of the world. The Holy Spirit is God and not just a force or energy. Salvation is by grace alone through faith.

- *Absolute behaviors* are behaviors specifically revealed in the Scriptures, especially the New Testament, as right or wrong for every Christian. They are not disputable matters. *Ephesians 4 and 5; Colossians 3*

Non-absolutes are not essential to the Christian faith. They can change over time, and can be different in various cultures and time periods.

- Non-absolutes are the disputable matters. Examples in Romans 14 are food, drink, and religious celebrations. These are neutral—neither right nor wrong in themselves.

- As a Christian, you are free to determine between you and Jesus His will for you on those issues. Ask Jesus to give us guidance on a disputable matter and emerge with either *personal convictions* or *preferences*.

- Jesus may give you a *personal conviction* about something that is right or wrong for you individually. Then, you must live by that conviction, even though other believers may differ. If you do not obey Him, Paul said that is sin for you. *Romans 14:5,14,22*

- *Preferences* are issues on which you may have a personal liking, but they are not right or wrong for you or for anyone else. These are usually traditions or customs.

- Starting with difference between absolutes and non-absolutes as the foundation, you can take any issue and follow a process to find out if it is a moral one. Gather the facts to find out if it is a moral issue addressed by Scripture. Then, consider how you respond biblically.

QUESTION 2: IS MY CHOICE STUNTING SOMEONE'S SPIRITUAL GROWTH?

- Principle #1: Regarding the non-absolutes, you may have the complete freedom to do something yourself, but it may not be beneficial to you or to those around you. *1 Corinthians 10:23*

- Principle #2: There is a distinction between public and private use of liberty. When your Christian brother or sister "sees you" and is distressed by what you are doing, that is a signal that you need to talk to Jesus about whether or not to do that activity, especially in front of them. *1 Corinthians 8:10*

QUESTION 3: IS IT DISRUPTING UNITY WITHIN THE BODY OF CHRIST?

- Romans 14:1 says, "accept him whose faith is weak." The Greek for "accept" means to "take to oneself, to receive with a special interest suggesting a welcome." There is an emphasis on community.

- You and I have a responsibility to contribute to and protect the love-bonded Christian community. But more than that, we are to remember who is Lord over our church community. It belongs to Jesus Christ, not to us. And He is not going to free us to exercise our liberty in such a way that will divide or cause dissension in His church over a non-absolute, disputable matter.

BALANCE YOUR LIBERTY WITH LOVE

- Talk to Jesus about any issue that comes up you do not know how to handle.

  ✓ Ask if the issue is a moral issue. If yes, God already tells you how to respond. If no, then talk to Jesus about it and determine what His will is for **you** on that issue.
  ✓ Ask if what you are doing or not doing is stunting someone's spiritual growth, including your own. If yes, don't do it in their presence until they are ready. If the answer is no, great! Enjoy your liberty. Either way, you are balancing liberty with love because you considered the other person first.
  ✓ Ask if the issue is disrupting unity in the Body of Christ, especially the local church. If yes, don't pursue it in such a way that will divide or cause dissension in His church over a non-absolute. If the answer to that question is no, great. Enjoy your liberty. Either way, you are balancing liberty with love because you considered the other believers first.

"In essentials, Unity, in non-essentials, Liberty, in all things, Love." (Martin Luther)

Let Jesus satisfy your heart with His grace so that your life overflows with His grace every day. You will experience a life of freedom and joy!

8: Grace-Centered Living

"I have been crucified with Christ and I no longer live, but Christ lives in me. The life I live in the body, I live by faith in the Son of God, who loved me and gave himself for me."
(GALATIANS 2:20)

Ask the Lord Jesus to speak to you through His Word each day. Tell Him you are listening.

DAY ONE STUDY

How are Christians meant to live?

God does not want believers to live by law, but by the Holy Spirit. Whether someone is living by law (God's Law or man-made laws) or by grace is determined by two key issues:

(1) The issue of **motivation:** Why you do what you do. Under law, a person works in order to *earn the acceptance of God.* Under grace, a person *trusts in Jesus Christ as her acceptance* and does good works out of love and gratitude.

(2) The issue of **power**: How you do what you do. Under law, a person lives from *her own power and resources.* Under grace, a person *lives by Christ's life and power* imparted by the Holy Spirit.

Life by the Holy Spirit is consistently presented in contrast to living by law.

1. Read Galatians 5:18. What does this verse declare?

2. Read 2 Corinthians 3:17. Where the Spirit of the Lord is, what is present?

3. Read Romans 7:5-6.

   • What results from the way of the written code (Law)?

   • Why have we been released from the Law?

Living by the Spirit is a new way of living for any human. Before Christ, you do not have that option. You lived according to your sinful nature. After trusting in Christ, you are freed to choose a new way of living—Spirit-led life. It is a much better way!

111

The Old Testament background of the ministry of the Holy Spirit

Who is the Holy Spirit? The Holy Spirit is **God himself**, the Third Person of what is called "the Trinity," a designation that also includes God the Father and God the Son (Jesus). You can review our study of the Trinity in Lesson 1, Day Four Study.

The Holy Spirit is described as possessing all the divine attributes and is referred to as God. It is important to remember that the Holy Spirit is a **Person**, not a "force" or merely an impersonal attribute or influence of God.

The Holy Spirit is described as having all the elements of personality: **intellect** (1 Cor. 2:11), **emotions** (Eph. 4:30), and **will** (1 Cor. 12:11). Personal pronouns are used of him, such as "he" or "him" (John 16:7-8). He is God.

The Holy Spirit was active throughout history from creation until the New Testament age.

4. Read Nehemiah 9:19-20, 30. In his prayer, Nehemiah recounts the role of the Spirit in the life of Israel as a nation. What was the Spirit's role?

5. How did the Holy Spirit empower ("anoint") the following individuals for special service?

   • Exodus 35:30-36:1—

   • 1 Samuel 10:1,6-9—

   • 1 Samuel 16:12-13—

The announcement of the Kingdom and the promise of the Spirit

The anointing of the Holy Spirit on Old Testament believers was not promised to believers of that time nor promised to be permanent when given. However, the prophets spoke of a future day, the time of the New Covenant or Kingdom.

6. Read the following verses. Mark everything promised about the Holy Spirit. Then answer the questions below.

And afterward, I will pour out my Spirit on all people. Your sons and daughters will prophesy, your old men will dream dreams, your young men will see visions. Even on my servants, both men and women, I will pour out my Spirit in those days. I will show wonders in the heavens and on the earth, blood and fire and billows of smoke. (Joel 2:28-30)

For I will take you out of the nations; I will gather you from all the countries and bring you back into your own land. I will sprinkle clean water on you, and you will be clean; I will cleanse you from all your impurities and from all your idols. I will give you a new heart and put a new spirit in you; I will remove from you your heart of stone and give you a heart of flesh. And I will put my Spirit in you and move you to follow my decrees and be careful to keep my laws. Then you will live in the land I gave your ancestors; you will be my people, and I will be your God. (Ezekiel 36:24-28)

And so John the Baptist appeared in the wilderness, preaching a baptism of repentance for the forgiveness of sins. The whole Judean countryside and all the people of Jerusalem went out to him. Confessing their sins, they were baptized by him in the Jordan River. John wore clothing made of camel's hair, with a leather belt around his waist, and he ate locusts and wild honey. And this was his message: "After me comes the one more powerful than I, the straps of whose sandals I am not worthy to stoop down and untie. I baptize you with water, but he will baptize you with the Holy Spirit." (Mark 1:4-8)

*   What did God promise about his Spirit in Joel 2:28-30?

*   What did God promise about his Spirit in Ezekiel 36:24-28?

*   What announcement did John the Baptist make about the Spirit in Mark 1:4-8?

When John the Baptist came on the scene just before Jesus ministry began, John declared that he would be baptizing people with water as a sign of their repentance from sin. But someone was coming after him who would baptize people with the Holy Spirit, thus identifying who were the people of God within whose hearts God would now dwell forever. This would be associated with God establishing his Kingdom on the earth. The time had come. God was ready to do what he had promised to do

The coming of the Spirit

7. Read John 3:5-8. What did Jesus promise about the Spirit?

113

8. Read John 7:37-39. What did Jesus promise to those who believe in him?

9. Read Acts 1:3-8. What did Jesus promise about the Spirit?

10. Read Acts 2:1-11, 32-41. How were the promises fulfilled in...?

- vv. 1-4

- v. 11

- v. 14

- v. 41

All of those promises from the Old Testament and from Jesus' own teaching were fulfilled on the day of Pentecost (50 days after the crucifixion). Many of Jesus' followers were gathered together praying. God responded by filling them with his Spirit in a very dramatic, recognizable, and unforgettable way. A new time had come. Peter preached a powerful sermon, urging the listeners to believe that Jesus was Christ the Lord. Three thousand were saved that day.

11. **Graceful Living:** Does the concept of the Holy Spirit's existence seem like science fiction to you? Like something out of a movie, e.g. "the force is with you" from *Star Wars*? We often feel this way because his name is more like a title. We have God the Father (we can relate to "father") and God the Son (whose name is Jesus, we can relate to "son" and "Jesus"). Paul often refers to the Spirit as the Spirit of Christ or God's Spirit to help us relate to him. Be honest with God here. Let him know how you feel. Ask him to help you trust what he says in his Word about his Spirit's presence.

Respond to God about what he has shown you today.

DAY TWO STUDY

The relational ministry of the Holy Spirit

When a person hears the Gospel and places her faith in Jesus Christ, several things happen instantaneously as a one-time event regarding the work of the Holy Spirit. These are a review and confirmation of what you have already learned about your identity in Christ.

12. Read Titus 3:4-5. At the moment of salvation (when one believes), what is done by the Holy Spirit?

13. Read Romans 8:9. What are the benefits of having the Spirit?

14. Read Romans 8:16. What does the Spirit reveal to us as believers?

At the moment of salvation, the Holy Spirit enacts rebirth and renewal to every new believer. In other words, you were born again and given life (regeneration). Don't you love how Paul describes this gift of the Spirit as "whom he poured out on us generously through Jesus Christ our Savior?" *Generously* is a purposeful word.

Our generous God gives his Spirit to live inside each believer and identify her as belonging to Christ. This is a declaration about our status with God and a promise of lasting relationship. *Belonging* reaches to our core need for love and security. Those without the Spirit do not belong to Christ. What a sad conclusion!

The Spirit also reveals to believers that they are now God's children. This is a ministry of the Spirit to us, enabling a new relationship with God as our Father, a loving Father.

Maybe you have not had such a great earthly father, but you have imagined what having a loving Father who delights in you as his child would be like. Your Father God is better than the best earthly father that you could ever imagine. You are the child of the living God. Woohoo!

15. At the moment of salvation (when one believes), what does the Spirit of God do for us?

- Galatians 4:4-7—

- 1 Corinthians 12:13—

- Ephesians 1:13-14—

God sent his Spirit into our hearts, teaching us to call out to God as our "Abba," which is more like the familiar "Daddy" or "Papa" rather than the formal "Father." We can talk to our God on the basis of our relationship with him as his child, someone who is dearly loved.

When we are individually baptized with the Spirit at the moment of our salvation, we are also baptized into the Body of Christ. Every believer who existed from the day the Spirit was given at Pentecost through the present time is a member of the Body of Christ, also known as the Church (capital "C"). We all share the same Spirit and the same relationship with both Christ as our Lord and God as our Father. This enhances our relationship with each other in the Body of Christ as well.

The Holy Spirit also places God's seal of ownership on us. The seal in Roman times represented the one in authority. Whatever seal the Spirit uses, God recognizes that as belonging to him. And he will fulfill all the promises he made to those who believe in his Son. The Spirit is a guarantee that when we die, we will be saved from God's judgment and given a place in God's heaven to dwell forever with God.

All of these wonderful things are part of the Holy Spirit's relational ministry to us. The Spirit does these for us instantaneously at the moment we place our faith in Jesus Christ. We do nothing. God does everything. We get to enjoy the relational benefits.

But wait. There's more...

16. Read the following verses. Mark what the Spirit does for us as believers. Then, answer the questions below.

    "If you love me, keep my commands. And I will ask the Father, and he will give you another advocate to help you and be with you forever—the Spirit of truth. The world cannot accept him, because it neither sees him nor knows him. But you know him, for he lives with you and will be in you. I will not leave you as orphans; I will come to you. Before long, the world will not see me anymore, but you will see me. Because I live, you also will live. On that day you will realize that I am in my Father, and you are in me, and I am in you." (John 14:15-20)

    "But the Advocate, the Holy Spirit, whom the Father will send in my name, will teach you all things and will remind you of everything I have said to you." (John 14:26)

    "I have much more to say to you, more than you can now bear. But when he, the Spirit of truth, comes, he will guide you into all the truth. He will not speak on his own; he will speak only what he hears, and he will tell you what is yet to come. He will glorify me because it is from me that he will receive what he will make known to you. All that belongs to the Father is mine. That is why I said the Spirit will receive from me what he will make known to you." (John 16:12-15)

- What is the Spirit's role for us according to John 14:15-20?

- What is the Spirit's role for us according to John 14:26?

- What is the Spirit's role for us according to John 16:12-15?

> **From the Greek:** "The Greek word translated "Helper" or "Counselor" in John 14:16 is *parakletos*. Both of these English words have connotations that are absent from the Greek word. Helper connotes an inferior, which the Holy Spirit is not. Counselor can call to mind a camp counselor or a marriage counselor whereas a legal counselor is more in harmony with the Greek idea. In secular contexts *parakletos* often referred to a legal assistant, an advocate, or simply a helper (e.g., a witness or a representative in court). The verbal form of this word, *parakaleo*, literally means to call alongside and, therefore, to encourage or to strengthen." (Dr. Tom Constable, *Constable's Notes on John*, pages 219-220)

Through the Holy Spirit, Jesus Christ has established with believers a relationship with himself similar to the one he enjoyed with the Father. Jesus said, "Don't you believe that I am in the Father, and that the Father is in Me?" (John 14:10). He then said that when the Holy Spirit comes, "On that day you will realize that I am in My Father, and **you are in Me, and I am in you**" (John 14:20). Authentic Christian living is when we live in the same relation to Jesus as he did with his father (faith, dependence). We trust; he supplies the life and power!

Your position *in Christ* ("you are in me") is your:

- Acceptance before God.
- Assurance of salvation.
- Identity.

Christ's presence *in you* ("I am in you") is:

- Life (regeneration).
- Power for living.
- The basis of a relationship.
- Promise and hope for our eternal future.

17. ***Graceful Living:*** Reflect on what these truths mean to you today.

117

DAY THREE STUDY

The empowering ministry of the Holy Spirit

From the beginning of our faith relationship with Jesus Christ, the Holy Spirit anoints us with God's presence and power. We need both to live the kind of life Jesus intends for us to live. After this one-time work of the Spirit to establish God's presence within us, he has an ongoing empowering ministry in the life of the believer.

18. According to Galatians 2:20, how is the Christian life to be lived?

19. Read Philippians 2:13 and Colossians 1:29. Who enables you to live the Christian life and how?

The genuine Christian life is to be lived by faith in Christ who is living in us. We are to yield our wills to God's work in us as he sees fit to work out his purpose in our lives. The work of Christ's power in us is far more powerful than our own. Our striving should be in sync with his work and purposes in our lives. **You are NOT left to be as good as you can be on your own.** What a relief!

20. From Acts 4:31, what does the Holy Spirit's filling empower the believer to do?

21. From Romans 5:5, what does the Holy Spirit empower the believer to have?

22. From Romans 8:26-27, what does the Holy Spirit do for the believer?

Focus on the Meaning: The Holy Spirit is the means by which Christ is "with us" and "in us" (Matthew 28:18-20; Galatians 2:20). Christ is in a glorified human body in heaven. He is with us by means of the Holy Spirit. To sum up: The ongoing ministry of the Holy Spirit has been well expressed by scholar Gordon D. Fee in the phrase, *"God's Empowering Presence."* (Gordon Fee, *God's Empowering Presence: The Holy Spirit in the Letters of Paul*)

23. Read the verses below. Mark everything related to what the Holy Spirit empowers us to do. Then, answer the questions below.

However, as it is written: "What no eye has seen, what no ear has heard, and what no human mind has conceived"—the things God has prepared for those who love him—these are the things God has revealed to us by his Spirit. The Spirit searches all things, even the deep things of God. For who knows a person's thoughts except their own spirit within them? In the same way no one knows the thoughts of God except the Spirit of God. What we have received is not the spirit of the world, but the Spirit who is from God, so that we may understand what God has freely given us. (1 Corinthians 2:9-12)

This is what we speak, not in words taught us by human wisdom but in words taught by the Spirit, explaining spiritual realities with Spirit-taught words. The person without the Spirit does not accept the things that come from the Spirit of God but considers them foolishness, and cannot understand them because they are discerned only through the Spirit. The person with the Spirit makes judgments about all things, but such a person is not subject to merely human judgments, for, "Who has known the mind of the Lord so as to instruct him?" But we have the mind of Christ. (1 Corinthians 2:13-16)

• From 1 Corinthians 2:9-12, what does the Holy Spirit empower the believer to do?

• From 1 Corinthians 2:13-16, what does the Holy Spirit empower the believer to do?

The Holy Spirit reveals to us the things that God has prepared for those who love him. We are empowered to understand what God has freely given us. The Spirit explains to us spiritual truth through his access to our minds. It is he who helps us to understand the Word of God when we read and study it. Many concepts in the Bible are foolishness to those without the Spirit. Thanks to the Spirit's empowering ministry, we are able to discern spiritual truth and understand how to apply it to our lives. And the most incredible statement of all is this, "We have the mind of Christ." All of this we receive because of the Holy Spirit's empowering presence in our lives.

24. What empowerment of the Holy Spirit is revealed in 1 Corinthians 12:4-11?

Scriptural Insight: The spiritual gift of "faith" is not referring to saving faith. For a good description of spiritual gifts, see "The Gifts of the Spirit" by Kenneth Boa at bible.org.

25. Read Ephesians 3:14-21.

- What does the Holy Spirit empower the believer to do in vv. 14-19?

- What is revealed about the Holy Spirit's power in vv. 20-21?

One of the greatest works of the Spirit in all believers is to strengthen us with his power so that we will know how dearly loved we are. Isn't it great to know this unbounded love for us and experience it so wonderfully? If that is not enough, Paul finishes off by saying that the Spirit fills us with the fullness of God. We have God's complete empowering presence in us giving us the kind of life that God wants us to know and experience. The Spirit's power is at work within us. He does more than we can ask or imagine for us with the end result that Jesus Christ gets the praise and glory!

26. *Graceful Living:* Briefly describe a great need that God has met in your life or a remarkable thing that God has done in your life through his Spirit's empowering presence in you.

Walking by the Spirit

The New Testament encourages believers to "walk by the Spirit" (Galatians 5:16), "live according to the Spirit" (Romans 8:5; Galatians 5:25) and be "led by the Spirit" (Romans 8:14; Galatians 5:18). The Greek word Paul used in Galatians 5:16 means to literally "walk"—a common idiom for how one conducts one's life or how one behaves, in this case one's faith walk.

What does it mean to walk by the Spirit? Walking by the Spirit means walking in submission to and dependence on the Spirit by faith. As Paul wrote in Romans 1:17,

> *"For in the gospel a righteousness from God is revealed, a righteousness that is by faith from first to last, just as it is written: 'The righteous will **live by faith**.'"*

We exercise faith in Jesus Christ for our salvation. We exercise faith for our daily living out the life of Christ within us. This daily faith walk by the Spirit involves every area of life.

27. Read Romans 8:5. What choice is made by those who live according to the Spirit?

28. According to Galatians 5:16, what will be true for those who choose to walk by or live by the Spirit?

At the beginning of this lesson, we stated that you can recognize if you are living by law or living by the Spirit based on two areas:

  (1) The issue of motivation: Why you do what you do. Under law, a person works in order to earn the acceptance of God. Under grace, a person trusts in Jesus Christ as his acceptance, and works from love and gratitude. **You know you are living by the Spirit when your response to God is to serve him out of your love for him and gratitude for what he has done for you.**

  (2) The issue of power: How you do what you do. Under law, a person lives from his own power and resources. Under grace, a person lives by Christ's life and power imparted by the Holy Spirit. **You know you are living by the Spirit when you are stepping out in obedience to God's Word, depending on God for the ability and power to do what he asks you to do, and trusting God with the results.**

29. *Graceful Living:* Do you recognize areas of your life—relationships, school, work, emotions, health, parenting, finances—where you are relying on your own power rather than the Spirit's power? Choose to give one of those to God and begin trusting in the Spirit's power. Which area will you choose? _____ Now live according to the Spirit and be led by the Spirit in that area of your life. Trust your God with the results and watch what happens!

Respond to God about what he has shown you today.

DAY FOUR STUDY

The filling of the Spirit (the fruit of walking by the Spirit)

The Holy Spirit connects us with Christ so that he is *with us* and *in us* forever—God's presence. The Holy Spirit empowers us to live the kind of life our God asks us to live—God's power. He is God's empowering presence. We are called to live by the Spirit, that is, to walk in submission to and dependence on the Spirit—by faith—daily.

30. Read Ephesians 5:18-21.

- What instruction does Paul give in v. 18?

- Why would the comparison to drunkenness be a good one?

- Paul referred to four of the many results of the Spirit's filling in Ephesians 5:19-21. What are they?

What does it mean to be "filled with the Spirit" (Ephesians 5:18)? The contrast between being filled with wine and filled with the Spirit is obvious. Both forces are internal. "Be filled"/ "Be being kept filled by the Spirit" amounts to letting the Holy Spirit who indwells us control us completely. We do this by trusting and obeying him as his Word directs. The wine that fills a person controls every area of her life as long as that person consumes it. Drunkenness results in ungodly behavior. Likewise, the believer who allows the Spirit to influence and direct her thinking and behavior will experience his control as long as she yield's her will to the Spirit. This is our ongoing responsibility (present tense), and it is expected of every Christian, not optional.

> **Focus on the Meaning:** Filling of the Spirit involves our **yielding** to God as God and yielding to his purposes and his truth. God fills what you open. Author Warren Wiersbe said this, "The baptism of the Spirit means that I belong to Christ's body. The filling of the Spirit means that my body belongs to Christ." (Adapted from *Dr. Constable's Notes on Ephesians*, page 61)

Outwardly, **a filled Christian is expressing joy of the Lord to others. Inwardly, she is expressing joy of the Lord to God himself.**

All that you learned so far about evidence of living by the Spirit would apply to evidence of being filled by the Spirit. Both result from yielding to and depending upon the Spirit's empowering presence in your life, choosing God's purposes and truth for your life. Both produce the characteristics of God's life in yours.

31. What Paul wrote in Colossians 3:12-17 describes more evidence of the Spirit's filling. Read the verses below. Note the evidences of being filled with the Spirit/living by the Spirit. Write what you find in each of the verses in the spaces below. These are evidences in your life of living by the Spirit.

- Verse 12—

- Verse 13—

- Verse 14—

- Verse 15—

- Verse 16—

- Verse 17—

Scriptural Insight: When he [Paul] speaks [in Ephesians 5:18] of being with the Spirit and when he speaks in Colossians of being under the rule of the peace of Christ and indwelt by the "word of Christ," he means to be under God's control. The effect of this control is essentially the same in both passages: a happy, mutual encouragement to praise God and a healthy, mutual relationship with people." (*NIV Study Bible,* note on Ephesians 5:18, page 1798)

32. In Galatians 5:22-23, what are similar evidences of living by the Spirit/being filled by the Spirit, which Paul calls "fruit of the Spirit?"

Think About It: We aren't able to produce the Christian life—only Christ can produce it. We are to maintain a dependent, receiving attitude—the same attitude of availability that Jesus presented to his Father for 33 years. And Christ will produce the fruit of his life in us. Our response should be, "Lord, I can't, but you can. (Bob George, *Classic Christianity*, page 177)

In the last lesson, I said that human parents raise their children to become more independent of them over time. But God raises his children to become more dependent on him over time. Living by the Spirit / being filled by the Spirit is dependent living.

33. **Graceful Living:** "The righteous will live by faith" (Romans 1:17). Living by faith is acting according to the Word of God, depending on Jesus Christ for the power, and trusting him with the results. From the evidences of living by the Spirit you discovered in the verses above, choose a few that you desire in your life. Now, ask Jesus Christ to produce these in you by saying for each one, "Lord Jesus, I can't, but you can. I want you to do this in my life. I trust you to do this in my life." Watch what he does!

The Holy Spirit's unseen presence

We cannot see the Holy Spirit inside of us. But we know he is working inside us because we become aware of the evidence. These are some of the things the Spirit does for us:

- **He helps us understand what the Bible teaches.** Has someone explained something to you about the Bible, and you understood what she was saying? That is the Spirit inside of you helping you to understand. *John 16:13; 1 Cor. 2:13*

- **He gives us the words to tell others about Jesus and say that Jesus is God.** Have you wanted to tell someone about Jesus but did not know what to say, then all of a sudden, the words just popped into your head for you to tell that person about Jesus? That is the Holy Spirit living inside of you prompting you with the right words to say. *John 14:26; 1 Corinthians 12:3*

- **He gives us assurance that we are God's children.** Have you ever felt really loved by God? That is the Spirit inside of you letting you know for sure that you are God's child, and He loves you. *Romans 8:16*

- **He makes us want to do what pleases God.** Do you have a desire to please God with your life? That is the Holy Spirit inside of you giving you that desire. *Romans 12:11; Jer. 33:31,33*

- **He helps us to feel joy as we serve Jesus and when we do the right things.** Have you ever felt really good when you chose to do the right thing or chose to be helpful? That is the Holy Spirit inside of you letting you feel God's pleasure. *Romans 14:17-18*

- **He makes us not want to do what does not please God.** Have you ever felt something tugging at you inside when you were tempted to do something wrong? That is the Holy Spirit living inside of you nudging you, reminding you what does not please God so you can choose not to do that. We can ask him to let us know in our thinking or feelings when we are tempted to do something bad. He promises to do that. *Galatians 5:16*

- **He makes us to become more like Jesus, especially in loving other people.** Have you ever started loving someone even more after you started praying for him/her? That is the Holy Spirit living inside of you doing that. *Galatians 5:22-23*

- **He makes us want to sing praises to God, in our hearts and out loud, and be thankful for God's goodness.** Do you like to sing praises to God? Do you feel thankful to God for his goodness to you? That is the Spirit living inside of you filling your heart with praise and thanksgiving to God. *Ephesians 5:18-20*

- **He prays for us when we need help or do not know how to pray.** Have you ever had a huge problem and did not know what to ask God to do about it, but God took care of the problem anyway? That is the Holy Spirit living inside of you working to take care of your need before you even ask. *Romans 8:26-27*

34. *Graceful Living:* Which of the evidences you just read have you recognized in your life? What other evidences of the Spirit have you seen? Thank God for specific ways and times his Spirit has worked in your life.

Respond to God about what he has shown you today.

Recommended: Listen to the podcast "Being Filled with the Spirit" after doing this lesson to reinforce what you have learned. Use the following listener guide.

Being Filled with the Spirit

THE FILLING OF THE SPIRIT

- Spirit Baptism occurs once, at salvation, as the Holy Spirit connects us with Christ so that He is **with us** and **in us** forever. Every Christian is permanently indwelled by the Holy Spirit and added to the Body of Christ. You have all of Him, not part of Him.

- After we are saved, the Holy Spirit living within us empowers us to live the kind of life our God desires for us to live. When we walk in submission to and dependence on the Spirit by faith daily, that leads to the filling of the Spirit.

  - ✓ The filling of the Spirit is **not** getting more of the Spirit inside of us. We have all of Him with His indwelling. It is also not something magical or mystical.
  - ✓ The filling of the Spirit **is** you choosing to be more influenced by God than by yourself or anything else.

- Paul's comparison of being filled with the Spirit to drunkenness is a metaphor (picture) of control that is internal. What things take control of you from the inside? *Ephesians 5:18*

  - ✓ Being filled with wine refers to excessive intake of alcohol which fills your bloodstream and influences every area of your life as long as you consume it. Drunkenness results in ungodly behavior. That is the fruit.
  - ✓ In the same way, when you trust and obey Jesus as His Word directs for you to do, the Holy Spirit will have more influence over every area of your life. Any Christian who allows the Spirit to influence and direct her thinking and behavior will experience His control as long as she yields her will to the Spirit. The results will be godly behavior. That is the fruit.

- Being filled with the Spirit is an ongoing choice and responsibility. We are to continually desire more of the Spirit's control in our lives and choose to give Him more control in our lives. He responds by doing it!

- Being filled with the Spirit is a privilege for every child of God. We do not earn it. God still chooses to do this to us based upon our responses to Him. It is a fruit of our dependence upon Him and yielding to His control in our lives.

THE DAILY CHOICE OF YIELDING

- Just like choosing to trust in Christ in the first place is a choice, staying dependent on Him after salvation is also a daily choice. *Romans 12:1-2*

- To yield to God means to give Him the right-of-way in your life. You yield to God at salvation, then continually yield to His Spirit's influence over your thoughts, attitudes, words, and deeds. Coming from your heart, you present your body as an act of worship. That is **yielding your body to God** for His control and purpose.

- **Yield your mind to God** by yielding to the Word of God. You yield your mind to God as you desire to know His truth through Bible reading and study of its teachings and truths.

- **Yield your will to the sovereignty of God and His will.** This may include submitting to one particular truth or command in the Word that you do not like. It may also include God bringing into your life situations or experiences that are not pleasant or desirable.

- Your body, your mind, your emotions, and your will belong to Christ. Yielding those to God is living dependently on Him. The fruit of living dependently is Spirit filling and all the Christ-like behavior the Holy Spirit will produce in your life.

THE FRUIT OF YIELDING

- When you choose daily to yield to the Spirit's influence instead of your own self-dependence, the Holy Spirit fills you with Himself. The Bible calls that kind of life choice, "walking by the Spirit" or "living by the Spirit."

- "Walking by the Spirit" or "being filled with the Spirit" means having a **conscious dependence** on the Holy Spirit. As you live the Christian life, face temptations, and make decisions, He uses that to transform your life to become more like that of Christ. The fruit of that is what we usually consider the fruit of the Spirit: love, joy, peace, patience, kindness, goodness, faithfulness, gentleness, and self-control. But it is a lot more. It is sharing Christ with others. It is courage and boldness and using God's Word to speak and convince others. It is being the visible representative of the invisible God.

- Our willingness to let the Spirit control and transform us requires us to recognize that we are weak to do anything of spiritual significance on our own. That goes against the western mindset that you must be strong on your own, stand on your own two feet. But our weakness is more useful to God than our self-determined strength.

  "God is attracted to weakness. He [responds to] those who humbly and honestly admit how desperately they need Him. Our weakness, in fact, makes room for His power." (Jim Cymbala, *Fresh Wind, Fresh Fire)*

- When you live in conscious dependence on Jesus Christ, choosing not to rely on yourself and your own strength, experiences or ideas, God's Spirit will fill you. Then, your thoughts, attitudes, words, and actions will reflect the life of Christ in you. And oh my, what comes from that will be graceful living for sure!

Let Jesus satisfy your heart with His grace so that your life overflows with His grace every day. You will experience a life of freedom and joy!

9: Grace-Motivated Obedience

"For the grace of God that brings salvation has appeared to all men. It [grace] teaches us to say 'No' to ungodliness and worldly passions, and to live self-controlled, upright and godly lives in this present age, while we wait for the blessed hope — the glorious appearing of our great God and Savior, Jesus Christ, who gave himself for us to redeem us from all wickedness and to purify for himself a people that are his very own, eager to do what is good." (TITUS 2:11-14)

Ask the Lord Jesus to speak to you through His Word each day. Tell Him you are listening.

DAY ONE STUDY

As you can see in the verses above, God's grace will teach you to say no to ungodly behavior and thoughts and to choose the way to live a godly life. You and I cannot obey God apart from Jesus Christ and his Spirit living inside of us. In fact, in John 15:5, Jesus told his disciples that they could do nothing fruitful that pleases God apart from staying connected to Jesus. Every day. All the time. That is the biblical view of Christian living while we are waiting for Jesus to return.

Life in the "Until" time

Any attempt to present a realistic and biblical view of Christian living must take into account where we fit in God's plan of history. We live in an overlapping age as we possess the life of the new creation to come through the Holy Spirit while still living in bodies of the old, fallen creation in a fallen, evil world. That puts us in an **already but not yet** tension. We are already justified in God's eyes, but we are not yet made sinless because we still commit sins. We are citizens of the kingdom, but the kingdom has not yet come to earth. Therefore, we need to understand Christian living in a way that **neither underestimates nor overestimates** the quality of life available to us in Jesus Christ.

- Those who **underestimate** the quality of life and power available to us through Jesus Christ and the giving of the Spirit will tend to approach Christian living legalistically with **self-confidence**. They believe they can accumulate Christian character through self-disciplined obedience (living by law). In other words, these believers revert to legalism in an attempt to perfect themselves.

- Those who **overestimate** the quality of life and power available through the Holy Spirit will tend to approach Christian living mystically (rather than rationally) with **self-confidence**. They believe that their possession of the "fullness of the Spirit" has lifted them beyond the power of sin in the flesh and beyond the power of evil present in the world. These believe that success, prosperity, and health belong to people of faith. To them, suffering, failure, and illness result from a lack of faith.

Both lead to what is called a "triumphalist" approach to spiritual growth, characterized by **confidence in self** and a dangerously low level of respect for one's sinful potential. Triumphalism is revealed by:

(1) A low-level of perceived need for Christ. His words, "apart from me you can do nothing" (John 15:5), have little meaning.

(2) The common response to our own failures or to the failures of other believers, "I can't believe I/he/she did that!" Shock that we still sin.

Added to the above wrong assumptions about the Christian life is the belief that the flesh improves and becomes "godly" over time, becoming less able to be tempted in the process, and reducing the need to depend on Christ. Christians who believe this are prime targets for failure, because they tend to play with fire and let down their guard against temptation.

This is the truth: **We *never* outgrow our need to depend 100% upon Jesus Christ.** Spiritual maturity is not reached by needing less of Jesus but by depending more on his truth and his power to live a life that brings glory to God and pleases him.

The conflict between the Spirit and the flesh

While we as redeemed and justified believers have new life in Christ, we retain our old bodies in which sin dwells (the flesh or sinful nature).

> **Focus on the Meaning:** What is the flesh? The term "flesh" (NIV: "sinful nature") refers to the *unredeemed* portion of our humanity—our bodies and souls through which indwelling sin assaults us. We do not know what it is, but we know how it works—sending messages to the mind that are in conflict with the Spirit. The flesh does not improve or change its nature over time as long as we are in our bodies! At the moment of salvation, we are born again of the Spirit. Our bodies are **not** born again, and our souls (mind, emotions, and will) are **not** instantly transformed. While the flesh does not improve, our choices can change over time as we learn to live by the Spirit (what you learned in Lesson 8).

1. What does Paul write in Romans 7:14-24 describing the experience of people who are trying to be good (on their own) yet are hampered by the flesh? Note: The context is applicable to believers and unbelievers alike. Those who refuse to see this as applicable to the believer are likely living in triumphalism.

Paul's words describe what happens when your mind wants to do what God wants, but your flesh refuses to cooperate. An old song says, "The flesh is such a pest."

2. What does James 4:1 say about our struggle with the flesh?

3. How does 1 Peter 2:11 add to our understanding of our struggle with the flesh?

4. In Galatians 5:16-18, how does Paul describe this continual conflict between the Spirit and the flesh?

Scriptural Insight: To live 'according to the flesh' is to live in keeping with the values and desires of life in the present age that stand in absolute contradiction to God and his ways...Paul is first thinking not about the several 'works' of the flesh he will soon describe, but as he will go on to explain in v. 17, about the basic perspective of life in the flesh. Such a perspective...radically opposes God and his ways, here designated as opposition to [living by] the Spirit. (Gordon D. Fee, *God's Empowering Presence: The Holy Spirit in the Letters of Paul*)

This opposition is with us every day. We must make a choice every day whether to give into living by the flesh or choose to live by the Spirit.

5. Read Galatians 5:19-26. Contrast the evidence of living by the flesh and living by the Spirit.

   Living by the flesh—

   Living by the Spirit—

6. Read the verses below. Using different colors of pens / pencils, mark the evidences of living by the flesh and the evidences of living by the Spirit. List what you find in the spaces below.

   Therefore each of you must put off falsehood and speak truthfully to your neighbor, for we are all members of one body. "In your anger do not sin": Do not let the sun go down while you are still angry, and do not give the devil a foothold. Anyone who has been stealing must steal no longer, but must work, doing something useful with their own hands, that they may have something to share with those in need. Do not let any unwholesome talk come out of your mouths, but only what is helpful for building others up according to their needs, that it may benefit those who listen. And do not grieve the Holy Spirit of God, with whom you were sealed for the day of redemption. Get rid of all bitterness, rage and anger, brawling and slander, along with every form of malice. Be kind and compassionate to one another, forgiving each other, just as in Christ God forgave you. (Ephesians 4:25-32)

   Follow God's example, therefore, as dearly loved children and walk in the way of love, just as Christ loved us and gave himself up for us as a fragrant offering and sacrifice to God. But among you there must not be even a hint of sexual immorality, or of any kind of impurity, or of greed, because these are improper for God's holy people. Nor should there be obscenity, foolish talk or coarse joking, which are out of place, but rather thanksgiving...For you were once darkness, but now you are light in the Lord. Live as children of light (for the fruit of the light consists in all goodness, righteousness and truth) and find out what pleases the Lord. (Ephesians 5:1-4, 8-10)

- From Ephesians 4:25-32, contrast the evidence of living by the flesh and living by the Spirit.

  Living by the flesh—

  Living by the Spirit—

- From Ephesians 5:1-4, 8-10, contrast the evidence of living by the flesh and living by the Spirit.

  Living by the flesh—

  Living by the Spirit—

7. From Colossians 3:5-14, contrast the evidence of living by the flesh and living by the Spirit.

   Living by the flesh—

   Living by the Spirit—

Think About It: Often, we blame people or circumstances for our anger. People and circumstances do not cause our anger, impatience, bitterness, etc. Our reactions to people and circumstances reveal where we are living—by the Spirit or by the flesh.

Although we no longer measure our way of living by the Law of Moses (including the Ten Commandments) which was given to Israel, the New Testament writers certainly gave us plenty of description of what sin looks like in a Christian's life! Living by the flesh is pretty ugly, isn't it? Would you say there is a stark contrast between the two lifestyles? The Christian life is not hard; it is impossible apart from Christ himself helping you do it.

8. *Graceful Living:* We all have areas of our own lives in which we are still living in the flesh. So do not feel alone. Which ones jumped out at you when you listed them? Jesus wants you to trust him to live by the Spirit in **those** areas.

Respond to God about what he has shown you today.

Day Two Study

Set free from the power of sin

Sin is ugly. Very ugly! Though we are a new creation in Christ, we still retain our old bodies in which sin dwells (the flesh or sinful nature). We are encouraged to live by the Spirit. Yet we are warned that we can choose to live by the flesh which is at war within us, at war against the Spirit. Are we left helpless like a pawn in the midst of the conflict? No, we have God's empowering presence in us. He is able to help us win the battle over sin. But we have a responsibility as well.

9. Read Galatians 5:16 and Romans 13:14. In order to live by the Spirit and not by the flesh, what is our responsibility?

Think About It: Paul wrote in Galatians 5:16, *"So I say, live by the Spirit, and you will not gratify the desire of the sinful nature."* Notice what this verse does **not** say. It does not say, "If you clean up the flesh, you will become spiritual" (the logic of legalism). It does not say, "The desires of the flesh will go away" (the logic of triumphalism). As long as we live in these unredeemed bodies, sin remains a source of temptation in us.

You can make the choice to not gratify the desires of the flesh but to walk by the Spirit, in dependence on the Spirit to help you follow through with this choice. Paul wrote in Romans 13:14 to not even think about how to gratify the desires of the flesh. Don't even go there!

But what does that look like? It helps to recognize and appreciate the power of sin.

10. Romans 6 is a discussion of life choices to serve God or to serve sin and the consequences of doing either. Let us see what advice God has for us through Paul. Read the verses below. Mark the choices we can make regarding sin and the consequences of those choices. Then, answer the questions below.

In the same way, count yourselves dead to sin but alive to God in Christ Jesus. Therefore do not let sin reign in your mortal body so that you obey its evil desires. Do not offer any part of yourself to sin as an instrument of wickedness, but rather offer yourselves to God as those who have been brought from death to life; and offer every part of yourself to him as an instrument of righteousness. For sin shall no longer be your master, because you are not under the law, but under grace. (Romans 6:11-14)

I am using an example from everyday life because of your human limitations. Just as you used to offer yourselves as slaves to impurity and to ever-increasing wickedness, so now offer yourselves as slaves to righteousness leading to holiness. When you were slaves to sin, you were free from the control of righteousness. What benefit did you reap at that time from the things you are now ashamed of? Those things result in death! But now that you have been set free from sin and have become slaves of God, the benefit you reap leads to holiness, and the result is eternal life. For the wages of sin is death, but the gift of God is eternal life in Christ Jesus our Lord. (Romans 6:19-23)

- What choices are identified for you (vv. 11-14)?

- What are the consequences of being slaves to sin (vv. 19-23)?

- What benefits do you reap from being slaves of God (vv. 19-23)?

In Romans 6, Paul personifies sin as a slave master—a power that enslaves us. Roman Christians understood this concept well as 1 out of every 2 people in the Roman Empire was a literal slave. We may not have a slave society any longer. But what we may not realize is that every human being has a master and is a servant to something—either God and his righteousness or sin and its wickedness—no neutral ground. You might think you are your own master, but you are not. Self is really following the voice of master sin within.

All of our lives before Christ, the old slave master sin called the shots. When we believe in Jesus, **a greater power moves in**—the Holy Spirit. He **sets us free from the power** of that old slave master to become what God intended us to be. But we are not set free to be our own masters. That is not what it means to be set free. Our options are still: 1) sin or 2) God. We have a new master, the one who set us free—Jesus Christ.

Jesus is our master, but the old slave master still calls my name and calls your name. That old slave master yells pretty loudly sometimes. And we listen! Yet, we do not have to listen or carry out its orders. We are freed from sin's power over us because a greater power has moved in—God's Spirit—one who woos us to do right. How we yield to God's Spirit working in our lives is our choice.

The advice God has for you through Paul is to consider yourself dead to sin but alive to God. Do not let sin reign or rule in your mortal body to obey it. Do not offer parts of your body to sin as instruments of wickedness. Instead, you have the ability to offer every part of your body to God as instruments of righteousness. Recognize that sin is no longer your master as it once was. Realize that you got nothing good out of wickedness, and see that you get great benefits from righteous living.

11. Paul told believers we are no longer under law (which only shows us what we do wrong. We are now under grace, which motivates us to do what is right out of love and gratitude for what God has done. According to Titus 2:11-12, what does grace teach us?

12. Read 1 Corinthians 10:13.

- What does God promise in 1 Corinthians 10:13 regarding temptation?

- Based on what you have learned already, through whom does God give us the way of escape—through ourselves or through the Spirit's empowering presence within us?

Whether or not we are presently tempted in a given area, we are capable of committing any sin mentioned in the Bible, given the right set of circumstances, time, and temptation. The progression may look like this:

#1. A received thought produces familiarity.

#2. Continued pondering produces a loss of repugnance and, eventually, curiosity.

#3. Desires, sometimes a total surprise, are generated to experiment. The most damaging or dangerous are the ones that blindside you with a desire you did not even know you could have done! So protect yourself at all times through prayer, "Lord, protect me from myself!"

#4. Having tried the activity, the flesh (like a goat) can learn to like, and even grow dependent, on any sensual stimulus.

Conclusion: We never outgrow our need to depend 100% upon Jesus Christ. Recognizing this should lead us to **have compassion on one another** (Galatians 6:1) and to **not take risks with sinful behavior!**

A habit is easier to maintain than it is to start. Faith can be a habit—a good habit. Make wise decisions to protect yourself, such as:

- Protect your mind. Desires of the flesh do not go away. They are, however, like a fire. They can burn hot or burn down, depending on whether you are feeding them.

- Do not play with fire. Make policy decisions (also called pre-decisions) to keep your distance from what tempts you.

   Think About It: Every believer has a choice. If something is causing you to stumble in your following of Jesus, you have the freedom to choose not to continue interacting with that thing. If it's political arguments, you can choose to stop engaging in political conversations. If it's pornography, you can turn off your computer. If it's money woes, you can choose the security of faith over the security of coin. The bottom line is, we have the power to remove obstacles and run a smooth race (Hebrews 12:1). I know several believers who feel 'trapped' in their sins and temptations. But God will always provide grace for sin and choice for temptation. There is always a way out of temptation (see 1 Corinthians 10:13). You just have to choose it. If you want to be mentally and emotionally free, that is. (John Newton, *Growing Young* blog, "Lessons Learned")

13. *Graceful Living:* Martin Luther, the priest whose actions initiated the Protestant Reformation in the 1500s, described it this way, "I cannot keep the birds from flying around my head; but by the grace of God I can keep them from building nests in my hair." What pre-decisions are you making or should you make to protect yourself from what tempts you?

Respond to God about what he has shown you today.

DAY THREE STUDY

Dealing with failure: "What should I do when I sin?"

How long do you think you can go without sinning, without doing something that is a work of the flesh? Six days? Six hours? Can most of us go 6 minutes without having impure thoughts or selfish behavior—unintentional and unrecognized? God understands this about us. Because we still retain our old bodies in which sin dwells, **we will sin**—unintentionally as well as deliberately. All sin is disobeying God, whether unintentional or deliberate.

But God knew that and provided for us even in those times of weakness. Let us review what we have learned to be true for us as believers.

14. What is true for anyone "in Christ" according to Romans 8:1?

15. What is true about our sins according to these verses?

- 2 Corinthians 5:19, 21—

- Ephesians 1:7—

- Colossians 2:13-14—

Praise God that all your sin is covered by Christ's work on the cross—whether unintentional or deliberate. All sin is forgiven before it is ever committed (you **have** forgiveness)—whether unintentional or deliberate. Your sins were nailed to the cross. There is now no condemnation for anyone in Christ Jesus because God is no longer counting your sins against you and has placed all of them on Jesus Christ. You receive his righteousness instead, making you perfectly acceptable to God.

16. Read Hebrews 4:15-16 and Romans 8:26. What assurance do you receive in these verses that God does not cut himself off from you when you are in a time of need?

God's throne is open to every believer for grace and help in our time of need, which certainly includes while we are weak from sin's influence. The Holy Spirit is interceding for us in our weakness, which includes sin. The Spirit does not stop speaking to us or working on us just because we do not want to listen.

Remembering who you are in Christ can help you recognize and avoid two errors in thinking regarding your sin that stem from the logic of legalism: 1) when you sin (regardless of what it is), God cuts off fellowship from you until you repent, and 2) a believer's sins build up until she confesses them and asks for forgiveness.

The first error in thinking ignores the fact that Christ is both *in us* and considers us *in him*. Nothing in our radical identity even opens the possibility of being alienated from God! If you are deliberately living by the flesh rather than by the Spirit in your life, you may choose to cut yourself off from praying to your God, reading the Bible, and community with other Christians. But that is not God cutting himself out of you. You belong to God forever.

The fruit of thinking that every time you sin you have broken your fellowship with God is tremendous guilt and insecurity. This is living by law rather than by grace. Because of what Christ did on the cross, we are set free from fear of God because of sin. We can bask in his amazing love and gratefully serve him.

The second error in thinking also is evidence of living by law. What is the fruit of teaching that our sins build up until we confess them to receive forgiveness? It is guilt, worry, and time spent trying to stay "confessed up." We envision God erasing the "not guilty" verdict on us and considering us "guilty" until we confess and are declared not guilty again. What is the difference between that and the Old Testament system of sacrifices where sins would build up between trips to the altar? Nothing!

Realistically, we probably won't recognize even half of our sins in a lifetime of being a believer. It is not biblical to think that we can do so and teach that we have to do So in order to maintain forgiveness or fellowship with God. By the way, just saying to God every day, "I confess all the sins I've done lately" is not what he is after. He is after a transformed life. That is why he went through all this trouble to give us a new identity.

Knowing you already have forgiveness leads to confidence, peace, joy and freedom. **Remember and rest** in your acceptance in Christ because of his finished work on the cross. And seek to live by the Spirit every day, which pleases the God who gave you this gift.

> ***Think About It:*** When we received the great exchange, we received Jesus' righteousness. Jesus received our sin. God decided this was how it would be 2,000 years ago. Sin does not mix with righteousness, does it? God does not erase Christ's righteousness from our account so he can add sin to it, does he? No! He gave us Jesus' righteousness permanently, knowing we could still sin. That means there is only one place for our sin to go. As soon as we sin, God removes it and puts it on Christ's account. That is what Paul teaches in 2 Corinthians 5. It is confirmed in 1 John 1:7 where John said believers are continually purified from sin.

17. Read Psalm 139:23-24. What should be your heart attitude toward God regarding sin in your life?

God wanted to remove the sin barrier between him and you permanently. He is interested in you spending your time and effort producing fruit for him to reflect his glory as he designed the human race to do. The righteous live by faith in a God whose grace defies anyone's attempt to still "measure up" (live by law) in some way. You should be thanking him daily for his forgiveness and his love and acceptance of you in Christ and the opportunity you have to live a radically different kind of life. What an outstanding privilege this new identity is!

Sin can no longer enslave you unwillingly because there is a **competing and greater power— God himself— in us**. Transforming power in your heart has set you free to produce his fruit. Living by the Spirit reveals to you through the Word and through prayer what is sin in your life and helps your repentant heart follow through with your desire for change.

The biblical process for dealing with recognized sin

Although our God does not hold our sin against us any longer, and his grace is continually forgiving us of sin, that does not give us permission to intentionally sin. Intentional sin does not fit with who you are as a forgiven Christian with a new life to enjoy.

But as long as we live in these earthly bodies, we will be tempted to sin. Sin will happen—whether intentionally or unintentionally. So as an already forgiven Christian, you might ask, "How do I deal with sin when I recognize it in my life?"

Great question. Here is the biblical process for dealing with sin as a believer:

Step One: View yourself rightly.

Your identity is not "_____" (coveter, greedy, gossiper, whatever that sin is).

> You are in Christ, a child of God, who sometimes "____" (covets, is greedy, gossips, makes immoral choices).

Step Two: Recognize (confess) the truth regarding your sin.

To confess biblically means *to agree with God about what you and he both know to be true.* Confession is not a formula, a process, or dependent on a mediator. Regarding sin in my life, it is not saying, "I'm sorry." It is saying, "I agree with you, God. I blew it!" You see your sin as something awful!

> Using sexual immorality as an example: While reading 1 Thessalonians 4:1-8, the Spirit convicts you that sexual immorality in any form is not pleasing to God. You are instructed to "flee/avoid immorality." You recognize this sin in your life. You agree with God that your immoral sexual behavior is seeking love and acceptance from the wrong source. It does not fit someone who knows God. That is confession.

Step Three: Confession is incomplete without repentance.

Repentance means *to change your mind about that sin, to turn away from it, to mourn its ugliness, resulting in changing your actions.* Paul said that godly sorrow brings repentance (2 Corinthians 7:9-11). Like the woman in Luke 7, it's saying, "I recognize what I am doing is wrong. This fills me with sorrow because it hurts You, God. Please help me to live differently." That is how our lives get transformed.

> For sexual immorality: You want to live in order to please God, and God wants you to avoid sexual immorality. So you pray, "Lord Jesus, please have your Spirit nudge me when I am not holy and honorable with my body. Help me to say no to temptation and

to give up any relationship that is not honorable to you. By faith, Lord, I want you to do that in my life." That is repentance.

Repentance is not repentance until you change something. You can confess "until the cows come home" (daily, habitually) and never change anything. Jesus called for people to "repent" not "confess."

Step Four: Repentance leads to dependence.

Depend on the living Christ inside you for that change to take place. Our Lord Jesus Christ is not interested in our compliance (outward conformity) as much as he desires our *obedience from the heart.*

> For sexual immorality: Memorize 1 Thessalonians 4:1-8 and any other scriptures that deal with staying pure and not rejecting God's instructions. Be sensitive to the Spirit's nudging when you are tempted to do otherwise. Choose to desire a life that pleases God.

18. *Graceful Living:* Is there any ugliness in your life that you mourn? Follow the steps above to live in freedom from that ugliness. What will you trust the living Christ inside you to do for you in that area?

Respond to God about what he has shown you today.

DAY FOUR STUDY

A realistic view of spiritual growth.

The Lord Jesus said he came to give us abundant life (John10:10), and the whole New Testament speaks in lavish terms about the quality of life God wants his children to experience. We are exhorted to press on to maturity in Christ. But how is spiritual growth recognized?

19. Read Ephesians 4:11-13. Christ gives the Church pastors and teachers for what purpose?

20. Read Hebrews 5:11-6:1.

- What does the writer of Hebrews say about someone who refuses to grow spiritually (vv. 11-13)?

- What does the writer of Hebrews say about our personal responsibility to grow spiritually (5:14-6:1)?

Focus on the Meaning: Spiritual growth is not growing 'more and more of me' so I need 'less and less of Christ.' It is growing in knowledge and experience as we walk with him, discovering more and more our need to depend totally on him.

Growth is gradual. There is a common misconception that one's life is either 100% "carnal'" (living by the flesh) or 100% "spiritual" (living by the Spirit) at any given time. In fact, probably every believer is trusting Christ with some aspects of his life *at the same time and right alongside other areas of his life where he is living in self-sufficiency.* Growth, therefore, involves Christ progressively teaching us to trust him in new unexplored areas of our lives, and deepening our sense of dependency in areas where we have previously grown a little.

You don't become more aware of your own "holiness" as you grow. On the contrary, the voices of the saints through history consistently agree that as you grow, you become more aware of *how far short you fall from true holiness.* You become *more* aware of your sinfulness as you grow, *not less.*

Understanding these things underscores our need to understand the grace of God in Jesus Christ, and our identity in him. Only because of the Lord's grace can we grow in self-knowledge and handle the ongoing struggle against the world, the flesh, and the devil. We would sooner or later throw in the towel without our assurance of his continued acceptance, teaching, and kindness. (Tim Stevenson, *T.E.A.M. Training,* Session 17)

We should all be committed to living by the Spirit and desiring all those good behaviors we saw in Day One of the last lesson—as committed as any legalist is to their set of rules. Spiritual growth involves God growing us, stretching us, and reconstructing us because he loves us and lives in us and desires that we be transformed into the likeness of his Son. It also involves our response of regular, diligent intake of God's Word and using it to train ourselves to become mature Christians who can distinguish good from evil. It is for our good and his glory!

Praise Jesus for working out your salvation in such a personal way. Feel free to use any creative way to reflect on your spiritual growth.

21. *Graceful Living:* Looking at your life, reflect on your growth over time.

- In what areas have you learned to trust Christ more?

- In what areas have you recently become more aware of your sinfulness?

Respond to God about what he has shown you today.

Recommended: Listen to the podcast "Graceful Living Is Dependent Living" after doing this lesson to reinforce what you have learned. Use the following listener guide.

Graceful Living Is Dependent Living

THE CALL TO BEING GOD-DEPENDENT

- God wants for us women to be God-dependent women. Not "independent except for when we need Him." But we are to be God-dependent all the time. The same is true of men. But being God-dependent all the time is so radically different from what our western culture has taught us most of our lives. From the time we are girls, we have been told that women should not depend on anyone or anything for our success.

- Are we as Christian women supposed to stay like babies not doing anything for ourselves? No! That is not what it means. We are supposed to grow and mature in our thinking and behavior.

- Are we as Christian women supposed to just lie back and let anything happen to us? No! That is not what it means. The New Testament teaches Christians to be wise and proactive in our dealings with everyone—whether in the church or outside of it—for our own good as well as for the good of others.

- Are we not supposed to use our skills, talents, advantages, and opportunities to be the best women we can be? No! That is not what it means. God wants us to give back to Him all those skills, talents, advantages, and opportunities He has given to us and use them for His glory. Submit those to Him for His purposes in your life.

DEPENDENT LIVING IS THE KEY TO BECOMING A GOD-DEPENDENT WOMAN

Human parents raise their children to be less dependent on them and more independent of them. But God raises His children to be less independent and more dependent on Him.

- The key to being a God-dependent woman is dependent living. Whatever He brings into our lives that makes us more dependent upon Him is good for us.

- Dependent living is not weakness. It is being stronger and having more influence, success, and satisfaction than you could ever have through your own efforts.

- As you submit to Him, our God uses our dependence on Him to transform us into the likeness of Christ.

BEING TRANSFORMED INTO THE LIKENESS OF CHRIST THROUGH DEPENDENT OBEDIENCE

There are two aspects of being transformed to the likeness of Christ. God's part and our part.

- God's part involves mystery about how He does it. The Scriptures teach that He works according to His will and purpose for your life. He puts everything in you to enable your transformation.

- Our part involves choices. 1) One choice is renewing your mind (Romans 12:2) through studying God's Words in the Bible to see how to approach life His way. The Holy Spirit uses the Word to transform you. 2) Another choice on your part is having a desire for God's work in you to give you the character of Christ. When you long for His work in your life, you will want to submit to what He is doing and ask for Him to change you. 3) A third choice is to commit to doing life God's way. That is part of the transformation process. Jesus modeled for us how to approach life God's way and how to live in dependence upon Him in the process. Living in dependence means you choose to trust Him in prayer.

- God will complete His part—both during your lifetime as you yield to His work in your life and after your life on earth ends as you begin your life in heaven.

GOD'S GRACE IS SUFFICIENT FOR DEPENDENT LIVING.

When Christ said to Paul that His grace was sufficient, He used a word meaning "to be possessed of unfailing strength, to be enough." God's grace is His unmerited favor toward humans. It is a gift from God that we do not deserve and can never earn.

- ✓ Salvation by faith alone through Christ alone is a gift of God's grace.
- ✓ The Holy Spirit's presence in every believer as a deposit guaranteeing our future inheritance of a perfected body and soul is a gift of God's grace.
- ✓ Being transformed into the likeness of Christ during this earthly life of ours is a gift of God's grace.
- ✓ All those wonderful treasures that come to us as new creations in Christ are gifts of God's grace. They are enough to make us into whatever God purposes for us to be.
- ✓ Every healing. Every answer to prayer. Every time we get guidance about what to do and where to go. Those are gifts of God's grace. They are sufficient to get us through this life and have joy in the process.
- ✓ The power of Christ works in us to help us in our weakness so that we can say with Paul, "I will boast all the more gladly about my weaknesses, so that Christ's power may rest on me." That is a gift of God's grace, sufficient to strengthen us and display the glory of Christ in our lives so that others are drawn to Him as they see it.

- When you admit that you are weak, you desire Christ's power to rest on you. That means to take possession of you. You desire for His power to act on your behalf. It is a heart change when you desire more of Him and less of yourself. The results will be the best for you and for those influenced by you for Christ's sake.

    Jesus Christ gave His life *for* you, so He could give His life *to* you, so He could live His life *through* you. (Major Ian Thomas, T*he Saving Life of Christ*)

- Dependent living is hard. It is being glad about weaknesses so Christ's power shines in you instead of your own. It is trusting Him for strength all the time, not just when you can't do something on your own power. It is loving God so much that you live your life in dependence upon Him which leads to obedience to Him. Graceful living is dependent living.

Let Jesus satisfy your heart with His grace so that your life overflows with His grace every day. You will experience a life of freedom and joy!

10: Grace Calls for You to Follow

"Whoever serves me must follow me; and where I am, my servant also will be. My Father will honor the one who serves me." (JOHN 12:26)

Ask the Lord Jesus to speak to you through His Word each day. Tell Him you are listening.

DAY ONE STUDY

Following Jesus as his disciple

1. Read Mark 5:18-19 and 10:52.

   - What do those who have been healed want to do?

   - Is this a typical response for those who have been healed of their sin and given new life today? Why or why not? Should it be?

2. Read Matthew 11:28-30. What does Jesus promise to those who follow him as his disciple?

Historical Insight: "Yoke" refers to the harness that connected a pair of animals, usually oxen, to a plow. The yoke linked them together so they could work efficiently. Often a young animal was paired with an older one, allowing the younger one to learn "on the job" from the experienced animal. In New Testament times, the phrase "take the yoke of" was used by the Jewish rabbis to mean, "become the pupil of a certain teacher," in this case the disciple of Jesus. (*Illustrated Dictionary of the Bible,* page 1066)

As we have seen so far in this study, the rest that Jesus offers is from the work of the Law (plus all the additional burdens Israel's spiritual leaders had loaded onto the people) in order **to maintain a right standing with God**. This invitation recalls Jeremiah 31:25 where Yahweh offered his people rest in the New Covenant ("I will refresh the weary and satisfy the faint"). Jesus, the revealer of God, invites those who long to know God and be refreshed in life to come to him. Jesus' burden is light compared to the loads Israel's religious leaders imposed on their disciples.

Both men who had been healed of their diseases and given new life wanted to follow Jesus. To follow means to follow where he is going and to learn from him. Jesus wants everyone who trusts in him as Savior and Lord to become one of his "disciples." A disciple is an active follower or learner. A disciple studies the teachings of another person whom they respect and applies those teachings to her life.

Focus on the Meaning: A great illustration of becoming a disciple of someone comes from the movie *Julie & Julia.* In it, a young woman named Julie Powell becomes a disciple of master chef Julia Child through Julia's cookbook, *Mastering the Art of French Cooking.* Julie Powell studies the recipes and follows the procedures. As a result, she experiences the joy of cooking and eating delicious food as Julia has taught her through a book. Towards the end, one realizes that Julie got to know Julia Child "personally" though they never met.

Jesus Christ calls you to **intentionally** follow him as his disciple. This means committing to learning from him and becoming like him as you obediently apply what he teaches you through his book, the Bible, and what he allows into your life. Have you made the decision to follow him?

3. Learning from Jesus involves being a student of his Word (our Bible) and choosing to put God's truth into practice as a lifestyle. Read the following verses. Mark the benefits of putting God's truth into practice and answer the questions below.

Therefore everyone who hears these words of mine and puts them into practice is like a wise man who built his house on the rock. The rain came down, the streams rose, and the winds blew and beat against that house; yet it did not fall, because it had its foundation on the rock. But everyone who hears these words of mine and does not put them into practice is like a foolish man who built his house on sand. The rain came down, the streams rose, and the winds blew and beat against that house, and it fell with a great crash. (Matthew 7:24-27)

To the Jews who had believed him, Jesus said, "If you hold to my teaching, you are really my disciples. Then you will know the truth, and the truth will set you free." (John 8:31-32)

So Christ himself gave the apostles, the prophets, the evangelists, the pastors and teachers, to equip his people for works of service, so that the body of Christ may be built up until we all reach unity in the faith and in the knowledge of the Son of God and become mature, attaining to the whole measure of the fullness of Christ. Then we will no longer be infants, tossed back and forth by the waves, and blown here and there by every wind of teaching and by the cunning and craftiness of people in their deceitful scheming. (Ephesians 4:11-14)

- What are the benefits of putting God's truth into practice (building on the rock) according to Matthew 7:24-27?

- From John 8:31-32, what are the benefits of learning from Jesus and applying what you learn?

- Based on Ephesians 4:11-14, what are the benefits of learning God's truth and putting it into practice?

The wonderful benefits of learning from Jesus and applying what you learn will enable you to withstand the storms of life. You will know truth and experience freedom from the bondage to error and all the chaos error can produce in your life. You will no longer be tossed back and forth by every wind of teaching and the cunning ways of deceitful men or women. Peace, stability and strength will characterize your life regardless of circumstances. This stems from your choice to become Jesus' disciple.

Confidence in God's Word

Jesus knew the Old Testament scriptures well and used them in his life and ministry.

4. What did Peter say about the Word of God in the verses below?

- 1 Peter 1:23-25—

- 2 Peter 1:20-21—

- Why is this important?

Historical Insight: The Bible is an amazing book. It was written over a 1,500-year period by about 40 different authors living in several different countries. It was written in three different languages—Hebrew, Aramaic and Greek. Yet the Bible is consistent in its central theme and key figure. It focuses upon Jesus Christ. Such a feat would be impossible without one supreme Author—the Holy Spirit of God. We can have complete confidence in it!

5. What did the writer of Hebrews say about the Word of God in Hebrews 4:12?

6. In 2 Timothy 3:16, what did Paul declare about the Scriptures?

Paul said the Scriptures were God-breathed. That means what was written by people was breathed out by God. He spoke through men and women as his spokesmen. Peter said that the writers spoke from God as they were carried along by the Holy Spirit. God-breathed. God-driven.

Focus on the Meaning: God-breathed does not mean that the writers of the Scriptures were sleep-walking. What it means is that God used their personalities, their abilities, their understanding, their talents and the real-life situations they were in to bring forth the Scripture that he wanted. Most of the New Testament letters were written to deal with circumstances. God is perfectly able to work through real-life circumstances in a real-life person like Paul, for example, to bring about the end result that he intends to use for the next however many centuries for us. (Tim Stevenson, *TEAM Training,* Session 3)

In 1 Peter 2:2, Peter encouraged all believers to "long for the pure milk of the Word." Milk is essential food for a baby to grow and develop properly. Likewise, the Scriptures (Old Testament and New Testament) are essential food for every believer to grow and develop into maturity.

7. ***Graceful Living:*** Is this how you view the Scriptures—as essential food for your life? Do you long for the Word every day? Ask God to give you an insatiable longing for his Word and to draw you to himself through reading it.

Respond to God about what he has shown you today.

DAY TWO STUDY

Convictions based on God's Word

8. Read Colossians 2:8.

- What can take someone captive apart from Christ?

- What do you think Paul means? Give modern examples of hollow and deceptive philosophies that set up against the knowledge of God.

Do you want to be taken captive by such things? Of course not!

9. In order to not be taken captive by such philosophies, what should you do according to Romans 12:2?

10. Where does the Christian go to renew her mind? Online news sites? Talk show hosts? Social media posts? See what Jesus says in John 8:31-32. Where do you find his words?

11. What advice is given in 2 Corinthians 10:4-5 regarding what can take you captive and how to respond?

As we have seen in previous lessons, you renew your mind through knowing the Bible, which is God's truth (John 8:31-32), and through the Holy Spirit implanting that truth in your mind so you can understand it (1 Corinthians 2:9-16). With a firm hold on God's truth, you can diffuse arguments against the knowledge of God that are influencing you. And you can take captive your thoughts, making them obedient to Christ.

God and the devil agree on one thing: Both want to capture your *mind,* because whoever captures your mind will direct the course of your life. Everyone maintains a number of *premises* for living, both consciously and unconsciously. Premises are assumptions that form the foundation and shape of your thinking. They are important because of a universal law of logic and behavior: "If your premise is off, your findings will be off." The actions you take will not likely succeed.

God wants your values, beliefs, and convictions to be formed by his Word. Biblical convictions can be compared to the policies of an organization. Like policies:

- Convictions provide a measure of protection against danger by establishing safe boundaries.
- Convictions eliminate needless decision-making by settling many issues in advance, thereby enabling greater consistency, efficiency, and productivity.

Because biblical convictions are based on an objective standard of truth (the Word of God), they provide a reliable standard for daily decision-making, as opposed to living by fickle emotions.

12. According to John 14:26, what was the Holy Spirit's role in supervising the apostles' teaching and writing so that we may have confidence in the reliability of the New Testament?

13. What do Jesus' words about the Holy Spirit's work in John 16:12-15 add to our confidence in the reliability of the New Testament?

> **Scriptural Insight:** The apostles directly wrote 2 of the gospels and 6 other New Testament books. Mark is likely adapted from Peter's sermons.

14. What is truth according to Jesus in John 17:17?

The writings of the New Testament are the work of the Holy Spirit revealing himself to the apostles and other disciples of Jesus.

> **Historical Insight:** There are 5,686 Greek manuscripts in existence today for the New Testament. If we were to compare the number of New Testament manuscripts to other ancient writings, we find that...there are thousands more New Testament Greek manuscripts than any other ancient writing. The internal consistency of the New Testament documents is about 99.5% textually pure. That is an amazing accuracy. In addition, there are over 19,000 copies in the Syriac, Latin, Coptic, and Aramaic languages. The total supporting New Testament manuscript base is over 24,000...The Christian has substantially superior criteria for affirming the New Testament documents than he does for any other ancient writing. It is good evidence on which to base the trust in the reliability of the New Testament. (Matt Slick, "Manuscript evidence for superior New Testament reliability," http://carm.org/manuscript-evidence)

The historical reliability of the Scriptures is an important issue, and they (the Scriptures) can be investigated to show that the biblical records are trustworthy. Biblical convictions are based upon what God has revealed about himself. And we know that God's Word is true and reliable.

From our study so far, we know that the Bible asserts that humans can truly know God and know truth about him. However, our knowledge of God can never be complete. Deuteronomy 29:29 says this,

> *"The secret things belong to the LORD our God, but the things revealed **belong to us** and to our children forever, that we may follow all the words of this law."*

There will be things that you cannot know ("the secret things") or concepts you may not understand right now. You must humbly accept that. But we CAN KNOW what has been revealed. God has revealed in his Word much truth about him and his way of approaching life. Dwell on what you can know. Make your "home" there in your thoughts and guidance for living.

15. ***Graceful Living:*** We live in a world of controversy and diverse worldviews. Having an objective standard of truth can be both a shield and a weapon (Proverbs 30:5, 2 Corinthians 10:5). Do you have confidence in the reliability of the Scriptures? If you have come across certain parts of scripture that you do not understand or cannot know the answer, are you willing to humbly accept that?

Deeper Discoveries (optional): For more information on the reliability of the Scriptures as we have them in our Bibles, visit www.probe.org and www.bible.org. Search "reliability of the Bible."

16. ***Graceful Living:*** Considering Paul's advice in 2 Corinthians 10:5,

- Do you recognize certain areas of your thought life that you need to take captive and make obedient to Christ?

- What would it look like for you to take captive every thought and make it obedient to Christ?

- What could be the benefits to you when you take every thought captive and make it obedient to Christ?

Respond to God about what he has shown you today.

DAY THREE STUDY

Taking every thought captive

Living in intentional cooperation with the Spirit as he transforms you into the image of Christ involves the practice of "taking every thought captive" to Christ as exhorted by Paul in 2 Corinthians 10:5:

"We demolish arguments and every pretension that sets itself up against the knowledge of God, and we take captive every thought to make it obedient to Christ."

When you begin to understand this verse, you discover a few things.

- First, you need to pass everything that you believe, or that you think you should believe, through the grid of God's Word. Does it line up with the truth found in the Bible? God will help you recognize error in thinking.

- Second, you do not have to entertain every thought that runs through your head on a daily basis. Because the Holy Spirit lives in you, you have the ability to discern God-pleasing thoughts from thoughts that grieve his heart. You can take those grievous thoughts captive and replace them with truth from the Bible.

- Third, you do not have to be enslaved to emotions that are influenced by lies. The more you practice taking every thought captive to make it obedient to Christ, the freer you will be from the tyranny of your emotions. Your emotions will then be based on truth and will be beneficial to you.

- Fourth, error in thinking will seriously affect your behavior and your relationships. The more you practice taking every thought captive to make it obedient to Christ, the more you will be transformed by the Spirit into a godly man or woman whose life is filled with love, joy, peace and the rest of the fruit God wants to produce in your life.

The following are examples of questions commonly asked by people about different issues based on values, beliefs, and convictions. We are exhorted in 1 Peter 3:15 to always be ready to give answers to the hope that is within us. This hope comes from the truths we have learned that produce joy in our lives and draw more people to Jesus as we loyally follow him and tell others about him. Read the question and the common error in thinking. Comment on the effects of that thinking on someone's life. Look up the verses and determine what the truth is about that issue. Feel free to add other verses to derive your answer. Ask Jesus to help you understand the truth so you can be set free from error and provide answers to each particular question when asked by someone else.

17. **Question #1: Where can I find meaning & purpose in life?**

- *Error in thinking: Find it through people, places and things.* How does that thinking negatively affect a person's life?

- According to Ecclesiastes 2:1-11, what did Solomon learn about trying to find meaning and purpose in people, places, and things? See also vv. 24-26.

- What does Jesus say in John 17:3 that leads you to find meaning and purpose in life?

- How do the words in Ephesians 2:10 help us find meaning and purpose in life?

Think About It: You have made us and drawn us to yourself, and our heart is unquiet until it rests in you. (Augustine of Hippo, 4th century author of *The Confessions*)

- Where can anyone find meaning and purpose in life? The answer is…

18. **Issue #2: Are there objective standards of right and wrong?**
    - *Error in thinking:* Right and wrong are relative; there are no absolutes. How does that thinking negatively affect a person's life?

    - Based on Galatians 5:16-23, how do you know there are objective standards of right and wrong in God's eyes?

    Galatians 5 is only one list of behaviors God declares to be right or wrong. Add to that list the behaviors we have studied that are found in Colossians 3 and Ephesians 4-5. The God who created everyone has the right to make the rules.

    - Are there objective standards of right and wrong? The answer is…

19. **Issue #3: What is the source of human evil?**
    - *Error in thinking: It is the fault of others, or of circumstances.* How does that thinking negatively affect a person's life?

    - According to Mark 7:17-23, what is the source of human evil?

    - According to Jeremiah 17:9, what is true about the human heart?

Scriptural Insight: Scripture clearly teaches us that the real issues of life are spiritual and are really matters of the heart, the inner man. Maybe it's for this reason the word "heart" is found so many times in the Bible...When used metaphorically (depending on the context) *heart* refers to either the mind, the emotions, the will, to the sinful nature, *inclusively* to the total inner man, or simply to the person as a whole and is often translated as such...The term heart, then, generally speaks of **the inner person** and the spiritual life in all its various aspects. This multiple use of "heart" along with the way it is used strongly focuses our attention on the importance of the spiritual life. (J. Hampton Keathley, III, "Guarding Your Heart, accessed at www.bible.org)

- What is the source of human evil? The answer is...

20. **Issue #4: What if I choose to do wrong anyway?**

- *Error in thinking: I can do what I want without consequences.* How does that thinking negatively affect a person's life?

- According to Galatians 6:7-8, what will happen if you choose to do wrong anyway?

Think About It: For those who think they can do whatever they want without consequences, pride, coldness, and lack of compassion will characterize their lives. Their reasoning about whether someone gets hurt or not is, "It's not my problem. It is theirs." Other effects of this kind of wrong thinking are poor decision-making and a life of regret.

- What if you choose to do wrong anyway? The answer is...

21. **Issue #5: Where can I find success and security?**

- *Error in thinking: Find security in money and position. Seek success at any price.* How does that thinking negatively affect a person's life?

- What instruction did Jesus give in Matthew 6:31-33 about where you can find success and security?

- According to 1 Timothy 6:6-10, how can you find success and security?

- What are the dangers of seeking security and success through money?

Think About It: Money does not create nor maintain godliness. Contentment is a greater source of happiness and joy than prosperity ever could be.

- Where can you find success and security? The answer is…

22. **Issue #6: How can I become a person of influence?**

- *Error in thinking: Climb the ladder upward over people and circumstances.* How does that thinking negatively affect a person's life?

- What does Jesus say in Matthew 20:25-28 about how you can become a person of influence?

- What does Paul say in Acts 20:32-35 about how you can become a person of influence?

- How can you become a person of influence? The answer is…

23. *Graceful Living:* Challenge yourself to put 2 Corinthians 10:5 into practice.

- Review the 6 questions above. Ask Jesus to help you understand the truth for each one so you can be set free from error and provide answers to the questions when asked by someone else.

- What other issues affect you or other women that you know? Write them down and find verses to support the truth. Prepare an answer for each one of them.

Respond to God about what he has shown you today.

DAY FOUR STUDY

Surrender is a process—seek him, sit with him, and surrender to him.

In our society, you have so many options to obtain "knowledge" about how to live life—the education system, internet, television, movies, and books galore. Add to that whatever goes "viral." Facebook posts, Pinterest boards, and other social media outlets grab your attention. Everyone expresses her own opinion about the latest issue of life, and society says all opinions are equally valuable. From the last section, you realized that thinking not based on scriptural truth can lead to some disastrous results.

To grow spiritually, you must pursue your relationship with God through Jesus Christ. Remember, Christianity is Christ! You make the decision to not only be a believer but also Jesus' disciple—someone who follows him, learns from him, and leads others to do the same. Choosing to become Jesus' disciple means you choose to:

- Listen to his speaking voice through the Word. *Hebrews 4:12*

- Speak back to him from the heart in prayer. *1 Thessalonians 5:17*

- Maximize input of God's Word into your mind. *2 Timothy 3:14-17*

- Put truth into practice through obedience by faith. *James 1:22-25*

- Pursue relationships with other believers and disciples in the body of Christ. *Acts 2:42-47*

- Exercise your faith through serving others in Christ's name. *Philippians 2*

- Share your faith with nonbelievers and be willing to disciple new believers. *2 Timothy 2:2*

Purposely creating the time and space in our lives to sit with God allows him to nurture who we are as well as instruct us in what to do.

> **Think About It:** Jesus asked the rich young ruler to surrender his fortune in order to know true riches. He asked the young boy to surrender his meager lunch so that thousands could feast. He asked the disciples to surrender their plans, their dreams, their very lives, to follow him. And he asks us to surrender our rights, our reputation, our possessions, and our security. He wants our dreams and desires, our losses and our loves. Why? Because he knows that what he offers is better by far than anything we are holding onto. He knows that surrendering everything we have and everything we are to him yields joy, purpose and peace that we cannot possess any other way. He knows that when we put our pain, loss and regret into his loving hands we will finally begin to experience the healing and the hope we long for. (Woven, *The Truth about Redemption Next Step*, "Redeeming Hope: Your journey Toward Surrender")

24. **Graceful Living:** Are you willing to respond to the call of God's grace in your life to be more than just a believer but to become a true disciple of Jesus, learning from him and preparing yourself to lead others as well? Looking at the list above, what can you choose to do this week to become more of Jesus' disciple?

Respond to God about what he has shown you today.

Recommended: Listen to the podcast "Grasping Truth for Protection and Freedom" after doing this lesson to reinforce what you have learned. Use the following listener guide.

Grasping Truth for Protection and Freedom

Since the fall of humanity in the garden (Genesis 3), there has been a spiritual war raging in our world between God's truth and the lies resulting from human reasoning and demonic influence. One leads to overflowing joy and dependent living on God. The other leads to self-dependence and rebellion against God. This spiritual warfare takes captives. Believers can be taken captive by bad teaching.

> *For though we live in the world, we do not wage war as the world does. The weapons we fight with are not the weapons of the world. On the contrary, they have divine power to demolish strongholds. We demolish arguments and every pretension that sets itself up against the knowledge of God, and we take captive every thought to make it obedient to Christ. (2 Corinthians 10:3-5)*

RECOGNIZING SOMEONE WHO IS TAKEN CAPTIVE AWAY FROM CHRIST

- Influential fakers know how to get women to follow them. *2 Timothy 3:6-7*

- Women who never recognize and grasp biblical truth will be taken captive by whatever flashy teachings that come along and live unsatisfied, unstable lives. *Ephesians 4:14*

GRASPING TRUTH PROTECTS FROM ENEMY CAPTIVITY

- To protect yourself from enemy captivity, renew your mind through knowing the Bible, which is God's truth and through letting the Holy Spirit implant that truth in your mind so you can understand it. Then, you can diffuse arguments against the knowledge of God that are influencing you, and you can take captive your thoughts, making them obedient to Christ.

- The writings of the New Testament are historically reliable and, therefore, can be trusted.

- Grasping truth has three parts: First, you dwell in the truth of God you can know. Next, you humbly accept what you do not know or understand. And then, you discern any teaching that you read or hear through the complete revelation of God's Word.

DWELL IN TRUTH YOU CAN KNOW.

- To dwell in truth is to make your home there. That means God's truth dominates your thoughts and attitudes, governs your life, and satisfies your heart.

- God gives us plenty of truth in the Bible that we can know and trust. 66 books, 1189 chapters!

- God wants us to know the truth He has revealed to us, to make our home in that truth. *Ephesians 1:17-19*

HUMBLY ACCEPT WHAT YOU DON'T KNOW OR UNDERSTAND.

- Some things we read in the Bible we do not understand now but might in the future. There is much we can know now. But there are things we will never know or understand. *Deuteronomy 29:29*

- We can do our best to try to understand what is written. When you run across something that you cannot seem to understand from a Bible passage, make the choice to humbly accept what you do not know or understand.

DISCERN ALL TEACHING THROUGH THE COMPLETE REVELATION OF GOD'S WORD.

1. Evaluate what you read and hear by comparing it with the whole Bible.

- Read any verse in the context of the passage where it is found—the paragraph, the chapter, and the book.

- Examine the original words to see what the writer meant and what the audience likely understood.

- Look at other verses with similar content to let the Bible interpret itself. And you should always ask the Holy Spirit for understanding.

2. Avoid the "look-imagine-see dragon" when viewing any verse.

The "look-imagine-see" dragon shows up this way: someone *looks* at a verse or passage, *imagines* what they want it to say, then in their mind *sees* what they have imagined through twisting word meanings and interpretations. Once it starts, it is like a fiery dragon burning truth in its path. Cultural influence on Bible study feeds this dragon.

- Tame the "look-imagine-see dragon" by considering the Bible as sufficient on its own, not needing to be "improved."

- Tame the "look-imagine-see dragon" by basing your faith on what **is** in God's Word, not something you have just heard about it and not something you are imagining to be there.

- Tame the "look-imagine-see dragon" by following the inductive process for Bible Study—observation, interpretation, and application. Then, you can dwell in truth you can know.

The way to take every thought captive to Christ is to dwell in truth you can know, humbly accept what you do not know or understand, and discern all teaching through the complete revelation of God's Word. Grasping truth both protects you and preserves your freedom. Grasping truth leads to graceful living.

Let Jesus satisfy your heart with His grace so that your life overflows with His grace every day. You will experience a life of freedom and joy!

11: Become a Grace-Giver

May the God of hope fill you with all joy and peace as you trust in him, so that you may overflow with hope by the power of the Holy Spirit. (ROMANS 15:13)

Ask the Lord Jesus to speak to you through His Word each day. Tell Him you are listening.

DAY ONE STUDY

Jesus Christ calls believers to join in his work.

Jesus Christ gave his life for you by grace, so he could give his life to you by grace, so he could live his life through you by grace. Knowing Christ's love for you and the presence of his life in you should motivate you to "live for him" and to serve him through serving others. Both are responses to God's grace in your life. This would include letting HIs life in you overflow to others around you, particularly those who need to know Christ.

> **Think About It:** Often we embrace grace, and then live according to works. If we choose to celebrate his grace and ALL of its implications as part of our daily worship, we become people who experience incredible joy and freedom that we LONG to give away! (Judy Brower, *The Disciplemaking Ministry Guide for Women in Leadership,* "Navigate the Disciplemaking Pathway: Establish," page 30)

As you have seen through this study, Jesus Christ calls you to a new life through faith in him, clothes you with himself, commissions you with a purpose to live for him, and empowers you to fulfill that purpose through his indwelling Holy Spirit.

1. Read Matthew 9:36-38.

    *   How does Jesus feel about the crowds and why?

    *   What does Jesus declare to his disciples about the harvest?

    *   For what are his disciples to pray?

The evidences of human distress are everywhere around us. Women are in bondage to guilt, fear, destructive behavior, and fatigue due to the burden of responsibilities. Add to that erroneous views of God that leave them feeling empty, confused, and without meaning and purpose. Failure in relationships leaves women with a sense of rejection, worthlessness, and extreme loneliness. Jesus Christ's plan to meet that need for every woman is…himself.

2. Read Matthew 28:18-20.

- According to v. 18, what authority has Jesus been given?

- Because he has the authority to commission his followers, what specific work does Jesus commission his followers to do in Matthew vv. 19-20.

- What is his promise to them (v. 20)?

Jesus communicated his plan for meeting the spiritual needs of every person to his disciples in what is commonly called "the Great Commission." The Great Commission has one single focus: "Make *disciples.*" Jesus Christ chooses to accomplish the Great Commission through *people*— ordinary men and women like you and I as we are "going" about life sharing Christ by word and action to those around us, baptizing new believers as a symbolic proclamation of their new life inside, and teaching them who Christ is, what he accomplished on the cross for them, and how they can live out their new identity in him.

> **Historical Insight:** Men [and women] were his method. It all started with Jesus calling a few men to follow him. This revealed the direction his evangelistic strategy would take. *his concern was not with programs to reach the multitudes, but with men whom the multitudes would* follow...what is more revealing about these men is that at first, they do not impress us as being key men...Yet Jesus saw in these simple men the potential of leadership in the Kingdom. They were indeed 'unlearned and ignorant' according to the world's standard, but they were *teachable...*What is perhaps most significant about them was their sincere yearning for God and the realities of his life...Such men, pliable in the hands of the Master, could be molded into a new image— *Jesus can use anyone who wants to be used.* (Robert E. Coleman, *The Master Plan of Evangelism*)

Jesus Christ gave this work to his disciples—the very ones who watched him make disciples of them. They saw him do it! They knew what he was commissioning them to do. They experienced that relationship with him that changed their own lives. So they were willing to bring that experience to the lost, hurting, and hopeless people in their neighborhoods, cities, and destinations. They brought good news that was real, relevant, and life-giving.

As you have seen him change your own life, you can do this, also.

3. Read 2 Corinthians 3:2-3.

- What does Paul call those who have responded to the gospel through his teaching in Corinth?

- As a living "letter," how is this letter described?

- Who reads such a living "letter" (v. 2)?

Jesus chooses to have his followers tell his story—what he did for them and through them. In essence, you become a *living letter* of Christ (2 Corinthians 3:2-3). Your story illustrates the power of Christ in your life. Your story allows you to become a **grace-giver** as our Lord extended his grace to you. You have a story to share. Through sharing your story, you become a grace-giver to those who listen.

> **Focus on the Meaning:** People love to hear stories. This is evidenced by all the money that is spent watching movies, attending the theatre, buying books and by all the time that is spent watching the television. Telling your faith story is just that: your personal story about your faith. It's an unobtrusive way to speak about the love of God in your life and the love he has for all people…Your life and story is the best tract to be written! (*The Disciplemaking Ministry Guide for Women in Leadership,* "How to Share Your Faith," page 21)

4. *Graceful Living:* What has Jesus done in your life that you would not mind sharing with someone who wants to know?

Respond to God about what he has shown you today.

DAY TWO STUDY

Become a "grace-giver" through telling your story

There are several ways to look at telling your faith story. You may recall a dramatic event or specific point in time when you began a personal relationship with Jesus. So you remember well what it was like to not know him and the difference he made in your life.

Or you may have grown up in the church and feel like you always knew who God was and trusted in Jesus as your Savior as a child. Those who trusted in Jesus as children often feel they "have nothing to tell" because they do not have a dramatic story. Yet, in the case of childhood believers, there occurs a later, mature decision to follow Christ as his disciple where more obvious life changes occurred. If you are in this category, therefore, focus on that later turning point in telling your story—when you made the decision to follow Jesus as his disciple at some point in your teen years or adult life—a childlike faith that becomes an adult faith.

By the way, what you might consider "nothing to tell" except your faithfulness to Christ through the years is what every Christian parent wants for her child to tell. You have a story to share!

We will work on your story in stages. Today, you will recall your life before knowing Jesus or choosing to follow him.

Your Life before knowing Jesus or choosing to follow him

5. *Graceful Living:* Recall what your life was like before knowing Jesus or choosing to follow him. Use these prompts to help you.

    *   What were your attitudes, needs, and/or problems?

    *   From what did you get your security or happiness?

    *   How did those areas or activities begin to disappoint you or left you unsatisfied?

    *   To what source did you look for security, peace of mind, or happiness?

    *   What 2-3 words would you use to describe how you felt or what your greatest needs were at the time (e.g. loneliness, feelings of insignificance, anger, rejection)?

    *   Briefly share a personal example from your life that illustrates those needs and attitudes you just identified.

How you came to know Christ (point of salvation) or chose to follow him

You will continue working on your story to share with others. Now, you will recall what led to your knowing Christ or choosing to follow him.

6. *Graceful Living:* Recall how you came to know Christ (point of salvation) or chose to follow him. Use these prompts to help you.

- Share when and how you first heard the gospel and/or were exposed to knowing Christ.

- What brought you to the place of being willing to listen or of wanting to be more than just a believer?

- Who influenced you?

- How and when did you decide to follow Jesus?

- Describe how you felt, what truths you heard, what you thought about them, how you felt after you made the decision.

Respond to God about what he has shown you today.

DAY THREE STUDY

Your life since knowing Jesus and choosing to follow him

Not only is it important to share what brought you to Jesus but also to share how he has impacted your life. Offer hope to your listener. Today, you will recall the benefits you recognize in your life since knowing Jesus and choosing to follow him. This is the hope you offer to your listeners.

7. *Graceful Living:* Recall the benefits you recognize in your life since knowing Jesus and choosing to follow him. Use these prompts to help you.

- What conditions before you really knew Christ have been satisfied by a relationship with him?

- What does it look like in your life to have a relationship with Christ?

- How long did it take before you noticed changes?

- What does it look like in your life to have this closer relationship with Christ?

- What are your blessings since having Jesus in your life?

- Where do you struggle still?

- How do you depend on Jesus through those struggles?

- Briefly share a personal example from your life that illustrates the wonderful difference that Jesus Christ has made in your life.

Respond to God about what he has shown you today.

DAY FOUR STUDY

8. *Graceful Living:* Whether you like to be spontaneous or need everything written down, it helps to script what you will say. It forces you to think through what you will say to maintain your main idea. It helps you to manage your allowed time.

So put together what you have recalled in the past three days to develop something you can share in about 5 minutes. Spend only about 30% of the time on your "before," just enough to have them identify with your need at that time. Spend another 30% on the decision time, and spend the rest of the time on what knowing Christ has done for you. Always end inviting them to join your adventure. See "Ways to Explain the Gospel" at the end of this book.

Write it as you would speak it—shorter sentences, everyday words that are clear and simple. Include specific illustrations that give them snapshots of your life, not only general descriptions of your life events. Practice saying your story several times. Make eye contact with the listener to draw her into your story.

Write out your five-minute faith story. You can use the extra page at the end of this lesson.

Share your story

The night before he died, Jesus prayed in the garden for his disciples. He was confident they had received he truth of God and had believed in Jesus as the Son of God (John 17:6-9).

Jesus also prayed for all those who would believe through the message of his disciples.

> *As you sent me into the world, I have sent them into the world. For them I sanctify myself, that they too may be truly sanctified. My prayer is not for them alone. **I pray also for those who will believe in me through their message,** that all of them may be one, Father, just as you are in me and I am in you. May they also be in us so that the world may believe that you have sent me. (John 17:18-21)*

That prayer included those who heard their preaching in the first century A.D. as well as all those who have read their teaching written in the New Testament. True believers through the years have shared the gospel over the past 2000 years down to this day. You are one of those who have believed because men and women have shared the good news of Jesus Christ so that you could know Jesus and, therefore, know God well. Live intentionally as a GRACE-GIVER to those whom God places in your path.

9. *Graceful Living:* With whom would you like to share your story?

Ask God to give you opportunity to share your story of life with him. Courage and ability to share come through obedience. If you offer your story to Jesus and your willingness to share what he has done in your life, he will give you the courage to do so. This is another evidence of the grace God has given to you through Jesus Christ. Just say, "Yes!" and be ready.

Respond to God about what he has shown you today.

GRACEFUL LIVING—RECAP OF THIS STUDY

From the time sin entered into humanity's relationship with our Creator God, the one question that continually demands an answer is, "How can guilty sinful humans be made right in the eyes of a holy God?"

Our spiritual problem can be compared to death caused by a fatal disease: (1) Sin ("the disease" Romans 3:23—all sinned) and (2) Death ("result of the disease" Romans 6:23—wages of sin). Our twofold problem demanded a twofold solution:

- For the problem of sin, we need forgiveness and righteousness. *Answer: Christ's **death** on the cross.* We can now be cured of the disease.
- For the problem of death, we need regeneration (the restoration of **life**). *Answer: Christ's **resurrection** from the dead.* We can now be given life that is forever.

The ultimate grace gift came—Jesus Christ—providing an answer to both spiritual problems. This is the Good News, the Gospel.

The following quote by a 20th century Bible teacher captures the gospel message in a nutshell.

> Jesus Christ **laid down** his life **for** you...so that he could **give** his life **to** you...so that he could **live** his life **through** you. (Ian Thomas, *The Saving Life of Christ*)

Because of the cross, you can dwell on these FACTS because of your faith in Jesus Christ:

- God's wrath against sin was fully **satisfied** (propitiation) by Jesus' finished work on the cross.
- The barrier of sin has been taken away and complete **reconciliation** between you and God is possible.
- You have been purchased by the blood of Christ out of slavery and released into freedom as God's act of **redemption**.
- You are completely **forgiven** of your sins and that Jesus promises to cleanse your conscience from guilt.
- You have been declared righteous (**justified**) and are now perfectly acceptable to a holy God based on your faith in his son.
- God declares you holy because of your faith in Christ. You are **sanctified**—set apart by him and for him.

Because of the resurrection, you can dwell on the FACT that you are made alive by the indwelling Holy Spirit **(regeneration)** who unites you to Christ so that "Christ in you" is a fact of your new existence. You are born again as a new creation in Christ with a new identity in him.

With the restoration of life begins a new adventure. It was totally **God's work** to make sinners acceptable again in his sight. Our proper response is to **trust in his work**, to obey him because of our love for him and gratitude for what he has done, and to continually offer him our willing service.

Jesus Christ calls you to a new life, clothes you with himself, commissions you for a purpose (to be his disciple and to make disciples), and empowers you to fulfill that purpose through his Holy Spirit living inside of you.

"May the God of hope fill you with all joy and peace as you trust in him, so that you may overflow with hope (Romans 15:13)" while living this adventure of "Graceful Living" with Jesus today, tomorrow, and every future day of your life.

Recommended: Listen to the podcast "Graceful Living Leads to Fulfilling Your Purpose" after doing this lesson to reinforce what you have learned. Use the following listener guide.

Graceful Living Leads to Fulfilling Your Purpose

JESUS CALLS US TO A NEW LIFE WITH HIM.

- Christianity is Christ! It is about Jesus Christ and our relationship with Him.

JESUS CLOTHES US WITH HIMSELF.

- The moment we accept this call to new life, we get "clothed" with Christ (Galatians 3:27). This means that when God looks on us, He sees His own Son.

JESUS COMMISSIONS US WITH A TWO-FOLD PURPOSE.

- *First part of our purpose:* To follow Jesus as His disciple. To follow Jesus means to make the choice to learn from Jesus through what is taught in the Bible and to apply those teachings to your life. We do that through depending upon Him to help us be obedient to Him. The result is Jesus living His life through you, influencing those around you so they can experience His love as well.

- *Second part of our purpose:* To live as a disciple-maker. That means making disciples who make disciples who make disciples.

JESUS EMPOWERS US TO FULFILL THAT PURPOSE.

- His Spirit lives in us giving us the power to do what Jesus commissions us to do.

YOU CAN GET DISTRACTED FROM YOUR PURPOSE.

- We get distracted from our purpose by feelings of inadequacy, a fear of rejection, or desire for comfort in relationships. We get stuck in Bible Study and lose connection with those who do not know Jesus.

- This resulting sense of restlessness in you is a clue that you have been distracted away from your whole purpose. You are to be following Jesus as His disciple **while** living for Him as disciple-makers at the same time and with just as much intentionality.

THREE POWERFUL TOOLS HELP YOU FULFILL YOUR PURPOSE.

- *Tool #1:* The Holy Spirit at work in you and in the world.

- *Tool #2:* The gospel message. The Gospel is the good news about Jesus Christ coming to earth to save us from our sins. Christianity is Christ! It is all about a relationship with Him. If you have opportunity to tell someone one thing, tell her about Jesus.

- *Tool #3:* Your story. Sharing your story is a simple way to speak about God's love for you and how He works in your life. You can bring hope to someone who needs it. Just share what you know.

DISCIPLING NEW BELIEVERS IS ESSENTIAL.

Getting to know Jesus is the priority for new Christians.

- What they need first and foremost is to get to know Him well and be secure in their relationship with Him. Reading through the gospels is a great way to do that. They need to know Jesus first.

- All Christians whether new or old need to know some basics like who Jesus Christ is, what He did for them on the cross, what His resurrection means, and their new identity in Christ. They need to know how to live in freedom from the flesh because they can live by the Spirit's power. They need to learn to depend on the Lord and how that dependence leads to obedience to Him. They can get all that from our studies for beginners. Start out with *A Fresh Start,* a study designed especially for new Christians. Then, do *Painting the Portrait of Jesus,* which is a simple look at Jesus' life from the gospel of John.

FULFILLING YOUR PURPOSE AS A DISCIPLE-MAKER

- Not every Christian woman will become a director, coordinator, or small group leader. But every Christian woman from 15-95 can become a disciple-maker, sharing Christ and discipling new believers.

- Jesus satisfies your heart with purpose. He calls you to a new life, clothes you with Himself, commissions you with a purpose to follow Him as a disciple and to live for Him as a disciple-maker. Thankfully, Jesus does not leave you alone to work really hard to do what He has asked you to do. He empowers you to fulfill your purpose. The power comes from God's Spirit who lives inside you from the moment you trust in Christ for salvation.

- Your response is to live dependently on His power in your life by faith. You are simply to obey Him and trust His Spirit in you to work through you. And being a little scared is a good thing because you will rely on Him more. Feel free to say, "Lord Jesus, I can't do this on my own. I will trust you to do this in me and through me." Then, watch what He does! That is graceful living!

Let Jesus satisfy your heart with His grace so that your life overflows with His grace every day. You will experience a life of freedom and joy!

Small Group Discussion Guide

The following guide is designed for groups that meet for about 1½ hours or less. You will notice that some questions are skipped for the sake of time.

Ask the group to listen to the first podcast "The Promise of Graceful Living" before coming to the group. Help them find it by sending them a link to melanienewton.com/graceful-living.

INTRODUCTION

Start with prayer. Pray for the group to learn from Jesus what He wants them to know and to learn to love one another well to build our community.

Make sure everyone has a book, a schedule, and Bible / Bible app and knows how to use it. Ask if anyone is new to the Bible and plan to come alongside her during the week.

Get acquainted with each other. Ask a general question or two such as, "Share your name, where you live, and one thing you would like the group to know about you."

Introduce the study

- Look at the "Contents" page to see the lesson titles.

- Introduction page 1. Read the beginning paragraphs and "The Basic Study" section. Highlight useful online Bible study tools.

- Page 2: Tell them how to find the podcasts (melanienewton.com/podcasts or any podcast platform—search "Satisfied" by Melanie Newton, Season 9). Or you can read the blogs associated with the podcasts at melanienewton.com/blog.

- Read "New Testament Summary." The "Graceful Living" section tells this history of how a lecture course became this Bible Study.

- Page 3: Read the three paragraphs at the top of the page.

- Read "Discussion Group Guidelines." Add anything else pertinent to your group.

The Promise of Graceful Living Podcast

- Read through the listener guide on pages 5-6. Look up the referenced Bible verses and read them as you work through the guide.

- "The Promise of Graceful Living" section: The lessons will cover these bullet points in detail.

- Tell them to work on Lesson One for the next meeting.

Prayer

Recommendation: Listen to a worship song. Suggestion: "What a Beautiful Name It Is."

LESSON 1: CHRIST, THE GRACE-GIFT

Each lesson in this study covers several passages. Choose ahead of time which verses from the questions the group will read aloud as you proceed through the discussion. My recommendations of the ones that can be skipped are below. Also, some of the paragraphs that follow the questions just sum up what the verses revealed. You may choose to skip reading those.

Start with prayer. Read the verse at the top of the page.

Day One

- Read the 5th paragraph.
- Q1. Read "Focus on the Meaning."
- Q2. Read 2 paragraphs.
- Q3. Read "Focus on the Meaning."
- Read *Christianity is Christ*. Ask Q4.

Day Two

- Read the paragraphs bottom of page 9 and top of page 10.
- Q5. Skip reading the verses because they are on page 10.
- Q6. Avoid a rabbit trail about the demons going into the pigs. Focus on the authority of Jesus over them.
- Qs 7 & 8.

Day Three

- Q9. Skip reading the verses because they can be referenced on the page.
- Skip "Scriptural Insight" on page 14. Ask Q10. Skip paragraph.
- Qs11 & 12. Read the full paragraph at the top of page 15.
- Q13 and "Focus on the Meaning," which is the theme of the gospels. Cover Q14.

Day Four

- Q15.
- Read paragraph at top of page 17. Skip "Historical Insight."
- Q16. Skip "Historical Insight." Read paragraphs at top of page 18.
- Q17. Skip paragraphs that follow.
- Read paragraph on page 19 that follows the Nicene Creed. Cover Q18.

Other

- Discuss the podcast.
- Pray

Recommendation: Listen to a worship song. Suggestion: "What a Beautiful Name It Is."

LESSON 2: GRACE-COVERED SIN

Each lesson in this study covers several passages. Choose ahead of time which verses and teaching paragraphs the group will read aloud as you proceed through the discussion. My recommendations of the ones that can be skipped are below.

Start with prayer. Read the verse at the top of the page.

Day One

- Read the paragraphs under *Understanding the Gospel message*
- Q1.
- Q2. You can skip reading the Romans verses if they have done their lesson already.
- Qs3-5.
- Read the information on page 25 at the top about God's wrath. Make sure everyone understands this.
- Qs6 & 7.

Day Two

- Q8. Read Genesis 3:21 and Exodus 12:3, 5-6. Skip the Leviticus verses. Read the "Scriptural Insight."
- Q9. Skip reading Numbers 15:22-31.
- Qs10-12.

Day Three

- Qs13-15.
- Q16. Skip reading the verses and the "Think About It."
- Q17. Skip reading the verses since they are on the page.
- Q18.
- Qs19 & 20.

Day Four

- Q21. Read Romans 3:22-28.
- Qs22 & 23. Skip reading Ephesians 2:8-9. Discuss the "Think About It."
- Qs24 & 25. Read through the second verse. Use this worship song at the end.

Other

- Discuss the podcast.
- Pray

Recommendation: Listen to a worship song. Suggestion: "Before the Throne of God Above."

LESSON 3: GRACE TRIUMPHANT, PART 1

Each lesson in this study covers several passages. Choose ahead of time which verses and teaching paragraphs the group will read aloud as you proceed through the discussion. My recommendations of the ones that can be skipped are below.

Start with prayer. Read the verse at the top of the page.

Day One

- Make sure you read the last two paragraphs explaining the 6 terms.
- Read about Propitiation and cover Q1.
- Q2. Skip "Scriptural Insight" and cover Q3.
- Qs4 & 5. Skip "Scriptural Insight."
- Read all of *Satisfied...no longer angry*. Q6.

Day Two

- Read about Reconciliation and cover Qs7 & 8.
- Qs9 & 10. Skip "Scriptural Insight."
- Q11. Read *Restored...no longer broken*. Skip Q12. Cover Q13.

Day Three

- Read about Redemption and cover Qs14 & 15. Skip reading Mark 10:45.
- Qs16 & 17. Skip "Scriptural Insight."
- Qs 18 & 19.
- Q20. Skip reading verses.
- Cover *Released...no longer in bondage* section and Q21 (optional).

Day Four

- Skip the two paragraphs at the top of the page. Cover Q22.

Other

- The podcast is a recap of the lesson.
- Pray

Recommendation: Listen to a worship song. Suggestion: "In Christ Alone."

LESSON 4: GRACE TRIUMPHANT, PART 2

Each lesson in this study covers several passages. Choose ahead of time which verses and teaching paragraphs the group will read aloud as you proceed through the discussion. My recommendations of the ones that can be skipped are below.

Start with prayer. Read the verse at the top of the page.

Day One

- Review the three words from the last lesson.
- Read about Forgiveness. Q1. Skip reading Hebrews 9:22.
- Qs2 & 3.
- Qs4-9.
- Read *Forgiven…no longer burdened.*
- Cover the truth in Q10. Ask Q11.

Day Two

- Read about Justification. Q12. Read the verses on the page.
- Skip both "Scriptural Insight" sections on page 56. Read the rest of the page. Do Q13.
- Q14. Skip reading Romans 5:10. Qs15-17. Skip "Focus on the Meaning."
- Read *Righteous…no longer guilty.* Q18 if appropriate for your group.

Day Three

- Read about Sanctification. Qs19-21.
- Q22. Skip reading the verses in that question. Read "Focus on the Meaning."
- Q23.
- Read *Perfected…no longer flawed.* Q24.

Day Four

- Read first full paragraph on top of page 62.
- Q25.

Other

- * The podcast is a recap of the lesson.
- * Pray

Recommendation: Listen to a worship song. Suggestion: "Amazing Love" (You Are My King).

LESSON 5: GRACE-GIVEN LIFE TO YOU

Each lesson in this study covers several passages. Choose ahead of time which verses and teaching paragraphs the group will read aloud as you proceed through the discussion. My recommendations of the ones that can be skipped are below.

Start with prayer. Read the verse at the top of the page.

Day One

- Read the bottom half of page 67 from the quote onward.
- Q1. Read the rest of the page.
- Qs2 & 3. Skip reading Ephesians 2:1-3 and "Scriptural Insight." Read the rest of the page.
- Q4. Skip reading the verses.
- Read "Think About It" on top of page 71. Ask Q5.

Day Two

- Q6.
- Q7. Skip reading John 1:14 and Philippians 2:5-8.
- Qs8-11 and paragraph at the bottom of the page.
- Q12. Read "Dependent Living." Ask the questions that follow.

Day Three

- Read about Regeneration. Q13. Skip reading John 10:10.
- Q14. Skip reading Ephesians 2:4-5.
- Qs15-18 and paragraphs on this page.
- Q19 and first paragraph after the question.
- Read *Made alive...no longer dead.* Qs20 & 21.

Day Four

- Q22.

Other

* Discuss the podcast.

* Pray

Recommendation: Listen to a worship song. Suggestion: "In Christ Alone."

LESSON 6: GRACE-CREATED IDENTITY

Each lesson in this study covers several passages. Choose ahead of time which verses and teaching paragraphs the group will read aloud as you proceed through the discussion. My recommendations of the ones that can be skipped are below.

Start with prayer. Read the verse at the top of the page.

Day One

- Cover all of page 81 through top of page 82.
- Q1.
- Q2. Read 1 Corinthians 15:21-22 and Romans 5:12-14. Skip reading the rest.
- Read the information after Q2. Ask Q3.

Day Two

- Q4. Read Romans 6:1-11.
- Q5. Skip reading Ephesians 2:4-6.
- Read the paragraphs that follow Q5.
- Q6.

Day Three

- Read bottom of page 85 through top of page 86. You have covered this already.
- Q7. Read all the verses.
- Q8.
- Q9. Read all the verses.
- Q10.

Day Four

- Read first paragraph.
- Cover Q11.

Other

- Ask if anyone has questions from the podcast content. Try to stay away from a discussion about election versus free will.
- Pray

Recommendation: Listen to a worship song. Suggestion: "Amazing Love" (You Are my King).

LESSON 7: GRACE-BASED FREEDOM

Each lesson in this study covers several passages. Choose ahead of time which verses and teaching paragraphs the group will read aloud as you proceed through the discussion. My recommendations of the ones that can be skipped are below.

Legalism is a common experience for many Christians so there is more teaching in this lesson than the other ones. Unless your group is really into the Law of Moses, this guide suggests you skip most of what is covered in Days 1 and 2 so you can get to Days 3 and 4.

Start with prayer. Read the verse at the top of the page.

Day One

- Cover all of page 93.
- Skip "What is the Law?" section. Ask Q1. Skip reading the verses.
- Skip page 95 middle. Cover the last section "The giving of the Law…"
- Skip "Why was there a need for a New Covenant?" Ask Q3.

Day Two

- Q4. Skip reading the verses.
- Read the paragraphs on page 98 beginning with, "It is important to remember…"
- Skip Q5. Ask Qs6-8, reading the verses.
- Ask Qs 9 & 10. Skip reading the verses.
- Read the bottom of page 100 through top of page 101. If time, ask Q11.

Day Three

- Read top of page. Ask Q13.
- Q14. Read Colossians 2:16-23. Read the paragraphs at the top of page 103.
- Q15. Skip the paragraphs that follow if your group understands grace.
- Cover all of page 104, including Q16. Read the verses in that question.
- Q17. Read the verses and the paragraph that follows. Ask Q18.

Day Four

- Read the first paragraph. Ask Qs19-20, reading the verses.
- Q21. Skip reading Romans 6:1-7. Read the paragraphs that follow Q21.
- Qs22-24, reading the verses. Skip the "Think About It."
- Read the paragraphs at the bottom of page 107. Ask Q25.

Other

- Discuss the podcast.
- Pray

> **Recommendation:** Listen to a worship song. Suggestion: "In Christ Alone."

LESSON 8: GRACE-CENTERED LIVING

Each lesson in this study covers several passages. Choose ahead of time which verses and teaching paragraphs the group will read aloud as you proceed through the discussion. My recommendations of the ones that can be skipped are below.

Start with prayer. Read the verse at the top of the page.

Day One

- Read the first paragraphs as a review. Skip Qs1-3.
- Read top of page 112. Ask Qs4 & 5. Skip reading the verses.
- Q6. Skip reading the verses except for Mark 1:4-8 ("fire" relates to Acts 2)
- Q7. Skip reading the verses.
- Qs8 & 9. Read the verses.
- Q10. Just read the verses in the bullet points. Ask Q11.

Day Two

- Q12. Read Titus 3:4-5.
- Qs13 & 14. Skip reading the verses and the paragraphs that follow Q14.
- Q15. Just read Galatians 4:4-7 but not the others.
- Skip the paragraphs after Q15 on page 116. Ask Q16, reading all the verses.
- Read the rest of page 117. Ask Q17.

Day Three

- Read paragraph at top of the page. Ask Qs19-22, reading all the verses.
- Read "Focus on the Meaning" on page 119. Ask Q23, reading the verses.
- Skip the paragraph below Q23. Ask Q24, skip reading the verses.
- Q25. Rad the verses. Skip the paragraph that follows. Ask Q26.
- Read paragraphs at bottom of page 120. Ask Qs27 & 28, reading the verses.
- Read the rest of page 121, including Q29 if you have time.

Day Four

- Q30. Read the verses and the paragraphs that follow.
- Q31. Read the verses individually.
- Q32. Read the verses and the "Think About It" that follows.
- Q33 is personal. Try to cover the rest of page 124 to top of page 125 and Q 34, if time.

Other

- Discuss the podcast.
- Pray

Recommendation: Listen to a worship song. Suggestion: "Lord, I Need You."

LESSON 9: GRACE-MOTIVATED OBEDIENCE

Each lesson in this study covers several passages. Choose ahead of time which verses and teaching paragraphs the group will read aloud as you proceed through the discussion. My recommendations of the ones that can be skipped are below.

Start with prayer. Read the verse at the top of the page.

Day One

- Read "Life in the Until Time" through top of page 130.
- Read "Focus on the Meaning" page 130. Ask Q1. Skip reading the verses.
- Qs2 & 3. Read the verses.
- Qs4-6. Skip reading the verses and the "Scriptural Insight."
- Q6. Read the verses for each bullet point on page 132.
- Q7. Skip reading the verses. Read the "Think About It" on page 133 and Q8.

Day Two

- Q9. Skip Galatians 5:16. Read Romans 13:14 and "Think About It" that follows.
- Q10. Skip reading the verses.
- Read paragraphs top of page 135. Ask Qs11 & 12, reading the verses.
- Read the bottom of page 135 through top of page 136. Skip the "Think About It."
- Q13.

Day Three

- Read top paragraph on page 137. Qs14 & 15. Skip reading the verse.
- Q16. Read the verses and the paragraphs that follow. Skip the "Think About It" on page 138.
- Q17. Read the verses.
- Skip paragraphs at top of page 139. Read through all of "The biblical process for dealing with recognized sin."
- Q18 is personal.

Day Four

- Qs19 & 20. Read all the verses referenced.
- Ask what grabbed their attention from the "Focus on the Meaning" on page 141.
- Read the top of page 142. Ask Q21.

Other

- Discuss the podcast.
- Pray

Recommendation: Listen to a worship song. Suggestion: "Lord, I Need You."

LESSON 10: GRACE CALLS FOR YOU TO FOLLOW

Each lesson in this study covers several passages. Choose ahead of time which verses and teaching paragraphs the group will read aloud as you proceed through the discussion. My recommendations of the ones that can be skipped are below.

Start with prayer. Read the verse at the top of the page.

Day One

- Qs1 & 2. Read the verses and the paragraphs that follow.
- Read the "Focus on the Meaning" on page 146 and the paragraph that follows.
- Q3. Read only the Matthew verses.
- Skip paragraph top of page 147. Ask Qs4-6. Read all the verses and the "Historical Insight."
- Read bottom of page 147 through top of page 148. Ask Q7.

Day Two

- Qs8-11. Read all the verses.
- Read the paragraphs on page 149. Ask Q12, reading John 14:26.
- Qs13 & 14. Read the verses.
- Read "Historical Insights" and the paragraphs that follow on page 150.
- Qs15 & 16.

Day Three

- Read page 152. For Qs17-22, read all the verses. Derive your answers to "The answer is…" questions from the verses read.
- Skip "Scriptural Insight" on page 154.
- Q23.

Day Four

- Choose how much of this you want to read if you have time.
- Q24.

Other

- Discuss the podcast.
- Announce that next week will be story sharing time. They are to work on their faith stories following the prompts in Days 2 and 3. Then, they are to prepare a 5-minute version and practice it to share with the group. If you are doing this study on your own, prepare and practice your own 5-minute story to share when God gives you the opportunity.
- Pray

> **Recommendation:** Listen to a worship song. Suggestion: "He Lives" (I serve a risen Savior…).

LESSON 11: BECOME A GRACE-GIVER

Each lesson in this study covers several passages. Choose ahead of time which verses and teaching paragraphs the group will read aloud as you proceed through the discussion. My recommendations of the ones that can be skipped are below.

Start with prayer. Read the verse at the top of the page.

Day One

- Read all of page 161, including Q1. Read the verses.
- Qs2 & 3. Read the verses and the paragraphs between the questions.
- Read the paragraphs on top of page 163.

Days Two - Four

- Give everyone 5-6 minutes to share their story.
- If time, review pages 168-169, what they learned in this study.

Other

- Discuss the podcast.
- Pray

> **Recommendation:** Listen to a worship song. Suggestion: "He Lives" (I serve a risen Savior...).

The Believer's Identity in Christ

These benefits are yours from the moment you trusted in Jesus Christ for salvation. You are…

1 JUSTIFIED (DECLARED RIGHTEOUS) *"For all have sinned and fall short of the glory of God, and are **justified freely by his grace** through the redemption that came by Christ Jesus." (Romans 3:23-24)*

2 MADE AT PEACE WITH GOD *"Therefore, since we have been justified by faith, **we have peace with God** through our Lord Jesus Christ." (Romans 5:1)*

3 SAFE FROM THE WRATH OF GOD *"Since we have now been justified by his blood, **how much more shall we be saved from God's wrath through him.**" (Romans 5:9)*

4 RECONCILED TO GOD *"For if, when we were God's enemies, **we were reconciled to him through the death of his Son**, how much more, having been reconciled, shall we be saved through his life." (Romans 5:10)*

5 REDEEMED *"In him **we have redemption through his blood,** the forgiveness of sins, in accordance with the riches of God's grace." (Ephesians 1:7)*

6 FREED FROM CONDEMNATION (JUDGMENT) *"Therefore, there is now **no condemnation** for those who are in Christ Jesus." (Romans 8:1) "**Whoever believes in him is not condemned,** but whoever does not believe stands condemned already because he has not believed in the name of God's one and only Son." (John 3:18)*

7 INDWELT BY THE HOLY SPIRIT *"You, however, are controlled not by the sinful nature but by the Spirit, if the Spirit of God lives in you. And if anyone does not have the Spirit of Christ, he does not belong to Christ." (Romans 8:9)*

8 ADOPTED AS SONS *"because those who are led by the Spirit of God are sons of God…**you received the Spirit of sonship. And by him,** we cry out, 'Abba! Father!'" (Romans 8:14-15)*

9 ACCEPTED BY GOD *"Accept one another, then, **just as Christ accepted you**, in order to bring praise to God." (Romans 15:7)*

10 BAPTIZED INTO CHRIST'S BODY (THE CHURCH) *"For **we were all baptized by one Spirit into one body** —whether Jews or Greeks, slave or free — and we were all given the one Spirit to drink." (1 Corinthians 12:13)*

11 CHOSEN BY GOD *"For **he chose us in him** before the creation of the world to be holy and blameless in his sight." (Ephesians 1:4)*

12 SAVED BY GRACE *"For it is **by grace you have been saved,** though faith — and this not from yourselves, it is the gift of God — not by works, so that no one can boast." (Ephesians 2:8-9)*

13 GOD HAS BEEN PROPITIATED (SATISFIED) *"he is the **atoning sacrifice for our sins**, and not only for ours but also for the sins of the whole world." (1 John 2:2)*

14 FREED FROM THE LAW *"So my brothers, **you also were died to the Law** through the body of Christ, that you might belong to another, to him who was raised from the dead, that we might bear fruit to God." (Romans 7:4)*

15 TRANSLATED OUT OF DARKNESS INTO LIGHT *"For you were once darkness, but **now you are light in the Lord.** Live as children of light." (Ephesians 5:8)*

16 FORGIVEN *"When you were dead in your sins and in the uncircumcision of your sinful nature, God made you alive with Christ. He **forgave us all our sins**, having cancelled the written code, with its regulations, that was against us and that stood opposed to us; he took it away, nailing it to the cross." (Colossians 2:13-14)*

17 WASHED CLEAN *"And that is what some of you were. But **you were washed,** you were sanctified, you were justified in the name of the Lord Jesus Christ and by the Spirit of our God." (1 Corinthians 6:11)*

18 MADE HOLY AND BLAMELESS *"But now he has reconciled you by Christ's physical body through death to present you **holy in his sight, without blemish and free from accusation**…" (Colossians 1:22)*

19 SEALED IN CHRIST *"And you also were included in Christ when you heard the word of truth…Having believed, **you were marked in him with a seal, the promised Holy Spirit**, who is a deposit guaranteeing our inheritance until the redemption of those who are God's own possession…" (Ephesians 1:13-14)*

20 CLOTHED WITH CHRIST *"For all of you who were baptized into Christ have **clothed yourselves with Christ**." (Galatians 3:27)*

21	GIVEN CHRIST'S RIGHTEOUSNESS *"God made him who had no sin to be sin for us, so that **in him we might become the righteousness of God**." (2 Corinthians 5:21)*
22	MADE INTO A TEMPLE OF THE HOLY SPIRIT *"Do you not know that **your body is a temple of the Holy Spirit**, who is in you, whom you have received from God? You are not your own?" (1 Corinthians 6:19)*
23	MADE PERFECT FOREVER *"Because by one sacrifice he has **made perfect forever** those who are being made holy." (Hebrews 10:14)*
24	TRANSLATED OUT OF DEATH INTO LIFE *"I tell you the truth, whoever hears my word and believes in him who sent me **has eternal life** and will not be condemned; he **has crossed over from death into life**." (John 5:24) "As for you, you were **dead** in your transgressions and sins…But because of his great love for us, God, who is rich in mercy, **made us alive with Christ** even when we were **dead** in transgressions…" (Ephesians 2:1,4-5)*
25	BORN AGAIN *"Praise be to the God and Father of our Lord Jesus Christ! In his great mercy, **he has given us new birth** into a living hope through the resurrection of Jesus Christ from the dead." (1 Peter 1:3)*
26	SANCTIFIED (MADE HOLY) *"And by that will, **we have been made holy** through the sacrifice of the body of Jesus Christ once for all." (Hebrews 10:10) "And that is what some of you were. But you were washed, **you were sanctified**, you were justified in the name of the Lord Jesus Christ and by the Spirit of our God." (1 Cor. 6:11)*
27	MADE A NEW CREATION *"Therefore, if anyone is in Christ, **he is a new creation**; the old has gone, the new has come!" (2 Corinthians 5:17)* *"For we are **God's workmanship, created in Christ Jesus** to do good works, which God prepared in advance for us to do." (Ephesians 2:10)*
28	MADE CHILDREN OF GOD *"Yet to all who received him, to those who believed in his name, he gave the right to become **children of God**…" (John 1:12)*
29	MADE COMPLETE *"For in Christ all the fullness of the Deity lives in bodily form, **you have been given fullness in Christ**…" (Colossians 2:9-10)*
30	MADE HEIRS OF GOD *"Now if we are children, then **we are heirs — heirs of God and co-heirs with Christ**, if indeed we share in his sufferings in order that we may also share in his glory." (Rom. 8:17) "…since you are a son, **God has made you also an heir**." (Galatians 4:7)*
31	MADE CITIZENS OF HEAVEN *"But **our citizenship is in heaven**. And we eagerly await a Savior from there, the Lord Jesus Christ, who, by the power that enables him to bring everything under his control, will transform our lowly bodies so that they will be like his glorious body." (Philippians 3:20-21)*
32	MADE INTO A HOLY AND ROYAL PRIESTHOOD *"To him who loves us and has freed us from our sins by his blood, and has made us to be a **kingdom and priests to serve his God and Father…**" (Revelation 1:5b-6) "You also, like living stones, are being built into a spiritual house to be a **holy priesthood, offering spiritual sacrifices** acceptable to God through Jesus Christ . . . But you are a chosen people, a **royal priesthood**, a holy nation, a people belonging to God, that you may declare the praises of him who called you out of darkness into his wonderful light." (1 Pet. 2:5,9)*
33	GIVEN CONFIDENT ACCESS TO GOD *"In him and through faith in him **we may approach God with freedom and confidence**." (Ephesians 3:12) "Therefore, brothers, since **we have confidence to enter the Most Holy Place** by the blood of Jesus, by a new and living way opened for us through the curtain, that is, his body, and since we have a great priest over the house of God, **let us draw near to God with a sincere heart in full assurance of faith**, having our hearts sprinkled to cleanse us from a guilty conscience and having our bodies washed with pure water. Let us hold unswervingly to the hope we profess, for he who promised is faithful." (Heb. 10:19-23)*
34	WE HAVE BEEN GIVEN EVERY SPIRITUAL BLESSING *"Praise be the God and Father of our Lord Jesus Christ, who has blessed us in the heavenly realms with **every spiritual blessing** in Christ." (Ephesians 1:3) "his divine power has given us **everything we need for life and godliness** through our knowledge of him who called us by his own glory and goodness." (2 Peter 1:3)*
35	NEVER SEPARATED FROM GOD'S LOVE *"For I am convinced that neither death nor life, neither angels nor demons, neither the present nor the future, nor any powers, neither height nor depth, nor anything else in all creation, **will be able to separate us** from the love of God that is in Christ Jesus our Lord." (Rom. 8:38-39)*
36	UNITED WITH CHRIST *"For if we have been **united** with him in a death like his, we will certainly also be **united** with him in a resurrection like his."*

Ways to Explain the Gospel

The following scripts will help you learn how to share the gospel with someone whenever the opportunity arises. Ask: "Has anyone introduced you to Jesus so you could know Him? May I?"

GOOD NEWS, BAD NEWS (EVANTELL.ORG)

1. The Bible contains both bad news and good news. The bad news is something about you and me, and the good news is something about God. Let's discuss the bad news first.

   Bad News #1—We are all sinners. Romans 3:23

   Bad News #2—The penalty for sin is death. Romans 6:23

2. Since there was no way you could come to God, the Bible says that God decided to come to you.

   Good News #1—Christ died for you. Romans 5:8

   Good News #2—You can be saved through faith in Christ. Ephesians 2:8-9

3. Is there anything keeping you from trusting Christ right now? Would you like to pray right now and tell God you are trusting His Son as your Savior?

BRIDGE TO LIFE (NAVIGATORS)

Use paper and pen for drawing the parts of the gospel message.

1. The Bible teaches that God loves all humans and wants them to know him. John 10:10; Romans 5:1

2. But humans have sinned against God and are separated from God and his love. Draw a chasm. This separation leads only to death and judgment. Romans 3:23; Isaiah 59:2

3. But there is a solution. Draw a bridge. Jesus Christ died on the cross for our sins (the bridge between humanity and God). 1 Peter 3:18; 1 Timothy 2:5; Romans 5:8

4. Only those who personally receive Jesus Christ into their lives, trusting Him to forgive their sins, can cross this bridge. Everyone must decide individually whether to receive Christ. John 3:16; John 5:24

FOUR SPIRITUAL LAWS (CRU)

1. God loves you and offers a wonderful plan for your life. John 3:16; 10:10

2. Humans are sinful and separated from God. Thus, they cannot know and experience God's love and plan for their lives. Romans 3:23; Romans 6:23

3. Jesus Christ is God's only provision for humanity's sin. Through Jesus, you can know and experience God's love and plan for your life. Romans 5:8; John 14:6

4. We must individually receive Jesus Christ as Savior and Lord, and then we can know and experience God's love and plan for our lives. John 1:12; Ephesians 2:8-9

USING JOHN 3:16

For God so loved the world that he gave his one and only Son, that whoever believes in him shall not perish but have eternal life.

1. **God loves:** *"For God loves you (name) so much…"* God is real. He loves you with an unconditional, never-ending love. He created you to have a relationship with Him. But we cannot experience this loving personal relationship because of sin in our lives. Sin is disobeying God. It puts a barrier between us and a holy God. No matter how hard you try, you cannot be good enough on your own to overcome this sin barrier. The penalty for sin is death. God's love had a plan…

2. **God gave:** *"God gave His one and only Son"* Jesus to live as a human without sin and then to take the penalty for our sin on Himself when He died on the cross. He was buried as a dead man then raised from the dead to be alive again so our sins could be forgiven.

3. **We believe God's love:** *"Whoever believes in Him."* Faith is trust. God asks that we trust in His plan, admit our sin and desire for a relationship with Him. Accept what Jesus did on the cross for us out of love.

4. **We receive what God gave:** *"Shall not perish but have eternal life."* To perish means to die separated from God and His love for you. Eternal life means you can enjoy a forever-family relationship with God and promise of living securely with Him now and after your life on earth ends. When offered a gift you want, you take it and say thank you. It is forever yours. Is there anything keeping you from trusting in Jesus right now?

HERE'S A PRAYER ANYONE CAN PRAY TO RECEIVE CHRIST:

Thank you, God, for loving me and for sending Your Son Jesus to die for my sins. I trust in Jesus Christ to be my personal Savior and turn my entire life over to You. Thank you for rescuing me and loving me as your child. Amen.

Sources

1. Augustine of Hippo, *The Confessions*

2. A.W. Tozer, *The Knowledge of the Holy*

3. Bob George, *Classic Christianity*

4. Charles Price, *Alive in Christ*

5. C.S. Lewis, *Mere Christianity*

6. Dr. Timothy Warner, *Resolving Spiritual Conflicts and Cross-Cultural Ministry, Freedom in Christ Ministries*

7. Dr. Tom Constable, *Constable's Notes on John*

8. Gordon Fee, *God's Empowering Presence: The Holy Spirit in the Letters of Paul*

9. Herbert Lockyear, Sr. Editor, *Illustrated Dictionary of the Bible*

10. J.B. Phillips, *Introduction to Letters to Young Churches*

11. John Calvin, *Calvin: Institutes of the Christian Religion*

12. John Hunter, *The Fall of Man*

13. John Newton, *Growing Young* blog, "Lessons Learned"

14. John R. W. Stott, *Understanding the Bible*

15. Martin Luther, comments on Romans 12

16. Matt Slick, "Manuscript evidence for superior New Testament reliability," accessed at http://carm.org/manuscript-evidence

17. Michelle Wallace, *"Fruit of the Vine: The Greatness of God," Living Magazine,* October 2012

18. *NIV Study Bible 1984 Edition*, Zondervan

19. N.T. Wright, *Jesus and the Victory of God: Christian Origins and the Question of God, Volume 2*

20. Oswald Chambers, *My Utmost for his Highest*, "The Staggering Question"

21. Philip Schaff, *history of the Christian Church, Volume 1*

22. Robert E. Coleman, *The Master Plan of Evangelism*

23. Tim Stevenson, *T.E.A.M. Training*

24. *The Disciplemaking Ministry Guide for Women in Leadership,* RESOUNDNOW

25. Tom Constable, *Dr. Constable's Notes on Romans*

26. *Vines Complete Expository Dictionary of Old and New Testament Words*

27. Woven, *The Truth about Redemption Next Step*, *"Redeeming Hope: Your journey Toward Surrender"*